Parenting
the *Heart* of
Your Child

Parenting
the *Heart* of
Your Child

DIANE MOORE

BETHANYHOUSE
Minneapolis, Minnesota

Published by Bethany House Publishers
11400 Hampshire Avenue South
Bloomington, Minnesota 55438

Bethany House Publishers is a division of
Baker Publishing Group, Grand Rapids, Michigan.

Printed in the United States of America

Library of Congress Cataloging-in-Publication Data

Moore, Diane (Diane Marie)
    Parenting the heart of your child : teaching your kids to make good decisions even when no one is looking / by Diane Moore.
        p. cm.
    Summary: "Discover Biblically sound keys to raising morally mature children that focus on character development, not just following rules"—Provided by publisher.
    ISBN 0-7642-0036-4 (pbk.)
    1. Child rearing—Religious aspects—Christianity. 2. Parenting—Religious aspects—Christianity. 3. Moral development. 4. Decision making in children. I. Title.

    HQ769.3.M66   2005
    248.8'45—dc22
                                                                            2005004888

Acknowledgments

A special thanks to Rob, my husband and best friend, who told me the second week of our marriage that he felt his duty as a husband was to help me be the best "me" I could possibly be . . . and he has spent our entire married years doing just that!

Together we dedicate this book to my parents, Jim and Martha Myers, whose extravagant love and support have taken this book from just a good idea to the paper and ink you hold in your hands today. Thanks, Dad, for reminding me every time I got distracted with other projects: "Di, just write the book."

To my wonderful friends and family who generously supported my ministry through Youth for Christ: Thank you for believing in the importance of ministry to families.

To Marilyn, who slept while I wrote a good portion of this book: I'm so glad you woke up.

DIANE MOORE is the Executive Director for Healthy Families International, a teaching, coaching, and resource organization for parents. A popular and entertaining speaker, Diane loves to share *Parenting the Heart of Your Child* principles wherever she can. Besides regularly speaking to parents in a variety of settings, including public high schools and churches, and directly to students in middle schools, high schools, and colleges, Diane also provides family crisis counseling through the Portland, Oregon, branch of Youth for Christ.

A Certified Family Life Educator (CFLE), Diane holds a B.S. degree in Psychology (Family Studies) from Corban College (formerly Western Baptist College) in Salem, Oregon.

Diane is a wife and mother of three grown children: Corey, Joshua, and Robyn. She and her husband, Rob, live near Portland, Oregon, with their cat, Thunder, whose most endearing quality is that he thinks he's a dog.

You can contact Diane or find out more about Healthy Families International online at: *www.healthyfamiliesintl.org.*

Contents

Introduction

Now more than ever Christian parents need to be intentional about maturing the hearts of their children. It is disturbing to hear of statistics from trusted organizations that show kids in the church acting *the same* as kids in the world. This research undeniably shows that when it comes to moral behaviors such as premarital sex, drugs, suicide, etc., our kids are often not making the right decisions, regardless of the values they have supposedly been "taught."

The idea that our kids could grow up in homes that hold strong moral values and attend churches that vigorously teach the same values, yet not reflect those values in their decision making, compelled me to investigate and ultimately come up with the message of this book. What are we doing wrong? What can we do differently? What is keeping our children from connecting their professed faith to their everyday decisions?

In the early 1990s I saw a news report that was both intriguing and disturbing. A school district near our home had conducted an eleven-year research project with a unique anti-drug theme. Starting with a specific kindergarten class and continuing with that same group of kids for eleven years, they infused anti-drug curriculum into *every* subject *every* year until the students were tenth graders.

I heard about the program as the news media was reporting the shocking fact that when that particular group of students was tested in the tenth grade, it was found their drug usage had DOUBLED from that of the previous class of tenth graders, who had *not* received the extensive anti-drug messages!

What had gone wrong?

The best answer to that question came out of the mouth of one of the tenth graders. Interviewed when the story first broke, and asked why she thought drugs were such a problem for her and her classmates, she replied: "We heard so much about drugs and why we shouldn't use them that when the time came for us to rebel we thought, 'What could we do to rebel?' and drugs were the first thing to come to our minds."

From that perspective, the students had been *programmed* to do drugs!

After hearing the news report, I called that particular school district and was connected to the department in charge of the anti-drug program. I told them I was interested in using the data produced from that study and asked for a copy of the official results. They were offended by my inquiry and defensive of their program, declaring that the "results" did not necessarily mean the program was a failure! They essentially refused to release any information to me. Instead of using their failure to propel them to a greater understanding of how they could improve their outcome, they closed their files and blindly defended their program.

Closing our eyes to a problem never makes it go away. I tried it once in second grade when my teacher was mad at me for not finishing my homework. She came yelling down the aisle toward my desk, so I lifted my desktop and closed my eyes. I felt so much better . . . until she showed up at the side of my desk with smoke coming out of her ears!

Closing our eyes to our failure to stop the moral decline of our culture will not help us. We will only continue to spend all of our energy and money on techniques and programs that are not effective in helping students develop moral character. A fresh perspective is needed before we can successfully bring about changes that *will* make a difference.

Obviously there has to be more to raising children who are mature in moral decision making than just teaching them ethics or having them memorize "right" and "wrong" behavior. In the failed school study, the program directors had taught anti-drug information to the *minds* of the children but had not factored in the role of the heart. It was rebellion that triggered the teenagers in the study to turn to drugs, and that rebellion did not originate in the mind. *Rebellion is a heart issue.*

I have come to believe that if we are ever to have an effect on the moral behavior of our children, we must deepen our focus to the heart level. It is not a matter of turning our focus *away* from teaching the mind or judging outward behavior but rather *deepening* our focus to include the complexity of what the heart is really thinking. The mind still needs vital information for good decision making, and outward behavior is still an important issue. Children can destroy their lives by choosing bad behavior! However, outward behavior needs to be seen as the *fruit* of the condition of the heart.

The Heart Is the Control Room for Outward Behaviors

The Bible abounds with illustrations about the heart and its importance.

- God is a God of people's *hearts* (Jeremiah 24:7).

- When we turn our life over to Christ we give Him our *heart* (Romans 10:9–10).

- When choosing David as king God informed Samuel that He doesn't look on the outside, He "looks at the *heart*" (1 Samuel 16:7, emphasis added).

- We reject God when our *hearts* are hardened (Hebrews 3:12–13).

From the beginning God has sought to reach and impact our hearts much more than just our minds and outward behavior.

- Jesus rebuked the Pharisees as people who "honor me with their lips, but their *hearts* are far from me" (Matthew 15:8, emphasis added).

- The two greatest outward signs the Jews performed, circumcision and burnt sacrifice, were deeply connected to the *heart* (Psalm 51:16–17; Romans 2:28–29).

All through the Bible the heart is described as being a core part of the decision-making process. Frequently people are described in the Bible as having "said in their *heart*" whatever decision they are about to make.

- When God gave Moses the Ten Commandments, His first instruction was that they were to "be upon your *hearts*" (Deuteronomy 6:6, emphasis added).

- Jesus said that adultery is committed in the *heart* first (Matthew 5:28).

- The Bible makes a direct link between the heart and outward behavior, asserting that outward behavior is merely a *fruit* of the *heart* (Luke 6:43–45; Matthew 12:33–37).

So . . . aha! It *is* all about the HEART. You knew it, didn't you? It's just that outward behaviors are so much quicker and easier to assess and monitor when working with children. It is simpler to educate and test the *mind*. To raise a child "at the heart level" is complex; it takes more time, effort, and skill. That's why I wanted to share the material in this book with you—to help navigate *my* children and *yours* to that deeper level of moral maturity that we know is God's desire for all of us.

While many people grieve when they see secularists remove important monuments like the Ten Commandments from public life, I am grieving and will continue to grieve until I see the Ten Commandments engraved on the *hearts* of our children.

As you consider the "secret path" the heart takes to maturity throughout this book, it is my prayer that you will be inspired and encouraged and, at the same time, receive extremely practical applications you can use immediately in your own family. I also pray you will be blessed with a greater understanding and appreciation of how God flawlessly works with His children.

Note: Study questions are available to enhance and apply each chapter's teaching. You can find them in the section called "Study Guide," which follows chapter eleven. Hopefully you'll find them helpful both in an individual study of the book and as discussion questions to share in a group setting.

CHAPTER 1

The Secret Path the Heart Takes to Maturity

I have always had questions about *why* God did some of the things He did in the Old Testament, questions that I guess I thought weren't polite or "Christian" to ask.

Questions like: *Why did God give the law "an eye for an eye, a tooth for a tooth," then do away with that law when Christ came? Why did God institute the lamb sacrifice and then later say He'd rather have obedience or mercy?*

As a child, I had big questions regarding the Old Testament sacrifices. I guessed that either God somehow needed the blood or maybe Satan needed it to satisfy some sort of bargain they had made. As a third-generation Christian, I didn't question this until I began to try to explain it to nonbelievers. Even to my ears it sounded . . . a little weird.

Another big question I had was, *Why did God take so long getting the law to His people?* He waited thousands of years, and it seems like He really took His time coming out against evils like polygamy and slavery.

And why did God form such a tight-knit club with His chosen people and then end up opening up the exclusive "club" to the entire world?

As a child I used to wonder if the reason God was changing tactics with His people was because He "learned" how to do it better as the centuries went by. How far from the truth this idea was! But we struggle with questions like these until we come to understand that our moral development doesn't happen all at once.

The Progression of Moral Development

God created us as developing creatures, and He condescends to deal with us at the level we are currently on, either as individuals or as nations. He knows we need to learn certain concepts before we can assimilate the next ones He wants to teach us. He knows His ways are so far above our ways that it will usually take us almost a lifetime of continual development to just *begin* to understand His ways. So He patiently works with us where we are, giving us what we need at the right time in order for us to discover the mystery of the profound love and grace He offers us.

When I began to look at this concept of spiritual development, I reasoned that if God *created* us as developing creatures, He would have worked with us accordingly. So we should be able to find evidence of His design for our moral development throughout the Old and New Testaments. In other words, the Bible would be a rich source of information about human development and parenting. Knowing what we needed for our spiritual formation, God would have communicated this to us through His word.

And the more I looked, the more I saw that this assumption was true. I believe the reason why our children are not making vital faith connections is because they are not maturing as God designed them to, and we as parents and leaders need to find out about His designs so we can cooperate with His desires for us and our children.

I figured that if there really was a progression leading to maturity in decision making, then it would be obvious in studying Scripture. Once I began this study I was amazed at what I found. I saw how God had worked throughout the Old Testament *morally developing* a nation to the point that they would be ready for Him to reveal His ultimate goal as unveiled in the New Testament.

I began to call what I was seeing in the recorded history of the Old and New Testaments "The Secret Path the Heart Takes to Maturity." As I started to apply the theory into different arenas of life, I realized what a remarkable tool it was for parents to use in rearing children better equipped to reliably make good decisions.

The true motives of the heart are cloaked deep within the soul of a person. The all-knowing God *searches* us to uncover the hidden motives of our hearts. Deciding to parent at this level might feel like you're trying to drive to a specific destination without a map or even marked roads!

You are probably asking the same question I did: *Wouldn't it be great if the heart matured in a predictable path that could be studied like a road map?*

Well, it does! That's why "The Secret Path the Heart Takes to Maturity" is so important for parents to know. I was shocked when I found it so clearly laid out throughout Scripture. God has always worked with people at their various stages of development, continually working to mature them to the higher stages.

The world's thinkers and researchers sometimes stumble onto the deep truths hidden in God's Word without even knowing it. Like so many other areas of life, this happened in the topic of human moral development. I'm referring to the work of a man named Lawrence Kohlberg, who used his opportunities as a leading psychologist to observe and document human behavior and decision making. Though he was not seeking God's truth, his findings tie in beautifully with what I uncovered in Scripture! He called his theory "the six stages of moral development."

It's exciting to know that truth exists in the world. It exists the same way a stone exists, whether people want to acknowledge it or not. Blind men or women can stumble over a stone of truth and record what they have found. Later, men and women who know God, who have spiritual insight from the Creator, can re-look at what the blind person recorded and see a much better picture of what was *really* found.

The Six Stages of Moral Development

A basic overview of the secret path the heart takes to maturity is organized under three main motivational levels with two stages in each:

Level One: *It's All About Me!*
    Stage 1—Fear of Punishment
    "I'm afraid of pain, failure, or being out of control."

    Stage 2—Anticipation of Reward
    "What's in it for me?"

Level Two: *It's All About Us!*
> Stage 3—Crude Conformity
> "I want to be accepted."

> Stage 4—Majority Rules
> "Is it normal?"

Level Three: *It's Bigger Than Us!*
> Stage 5—Self-Evident Truths
> "Is it the right thing to do?"

> Stage 6—Love and Truth
> "Does it express ultimate love and truth?"

The rest of this book is dedicated to describing in more detail this secret path the heart takes to maturity. The path is all about attitudes and deep inner motivations—the heart. For it is at this hidden level that good decision-making skills grow, mature, and then gradually change our outward behaviors.

Many times parents ask me what stage their child *should* be in based upon their biological age. I've always been reluctant to answer that question. The decision-making development process in an individual doesn't work as neatly and orderly as some of the other human development processes do. I see many parents in my counseling work who have teenagers that are stuck at Stage One. If I were to tell them that only toddlers should be at Stage One, it would be incredibly discouraging to them. I would like to encourage you to look at this system as a tool—not to assess and judge others, but as a means of assessing and using the information at each level to propel your child toward maturity. Where they start from at any age isn't as important as making steady progress forward!

MAKING THE JOURNEY

To make the journey from stage to stage more interesting, I thought it might be appealing to use the idea of people (children or adults) progressing from one island to another in their quest for spiritual and moral maturity.

The scenario goes like this:

- There are six different maturity STAGES from which people make decisions. The first four stages will be the islands laid out on a progressive path in the Caribbean Sea. (I thought I needed to make sure no one was visualizing anything Arctic!)

- Each island or stage is connected to the next one by a BRIDGE. Each bridge has two HANDRAILS.

- Each handrail represents an important focus or learning that must be mastered *before* the person can progress beyond that island (stage).

- The last two stages comprise the ultimate destination, the MAINLAND (which obviously doesn't have any handrails because it is the place we want to end up).

There are some presuppositions that need to be addressed before we dive into the details of the secret path of the heart. They are:

Presupposition One: All the stages are important.
Human beings are designed to continue to develop throughout their entire life-span. This is one element that *sets us apart* from all other creatures. The stages are developmental, with each stage building on the previous one, and each stage

is important. There are concepts that need to be gleaned from each stage in order for an individual to optimally develop. The early stages may seem uncivilized, but anyone who has had kids knows that they come out uncivilized. They need to be helped to become more civilized. The beginning stages, although crude, are as important to a human being's development as a foundation is to the structure of a house.

Presupposition Two: Don't try to jump too far ahead.

Kohlberg asserted that people understand moral decisions only up to *one stage beyond* the stage at which they are most often operating. This is important to understand if you are trying to motivate someone. Have you ever worked with someone who consistently misunderstood you? They misread your *dedication to diligence* for a *desire for power*, or your *kind acts* as *manipulative ploys*.

Why did they continue to misunderstand you? Maybe they were incapable of understanding someone who was motivated at such a wholly different stage from where they were operating. A teenager will often see the boundaries placed on them as cruel and controlling because they do not understand the reality of their parents' responsibility for their safety and well-being.

Higher stages need to be talked about and principles need to be taught, but it is important to keep track—on a *motivational level*—of where your child is currently operating. This means that as you are teaching younger children life principles, it is also appropriate to use the power of the anticipation of reward (Stage Two) as motivation. For older students it may be more effective to engage them relationally and make use of their desire to belong and be accepted (Stage Three).

Presupposition Three: Relationship is key!

This is the most important presupposition for parents to keep in mind, especially as we enter the next chapter on "fear of punishment" and see what crucial learning links take place in that stage. The Secret Path principles should be used by loving parents who are themselves operating at Level Three moral development. Parents should desire good relationships for their children—both with themselves and with God—more than simply behavior control. Tender nurture is the first foundation that must be laid in good parenting.

As we explore the different stages in this book, hopefully you will personalize the concepts and find *yourself* in the different stages. People at any point in their lives make decisions at various stages. No child or mature adult consistently makes *all* of his or her decisions in the same stage. But with honest contemplation, a person can discern the stage from which they most commonly launch the majority of their decisions. May you be inspired, as I have been, to stretch and grow in your own moral development as you guide your children to do the same.

Summary of Chapter One

- There is a knowable or predictable path people take to spiritual (moral) maturity.

- The specific progress on that path is identified by examining the *motives* behind decisions.

- Behind every outward behavior lies an inner motive. It is only by maturing the motive level that true growth and positive development can occur.

- The predictable path to maturity is not only evident in Scripture, but once understood, it also helps explain the differences between the Old and New Testaments.

- A simple look at the maturity path of inner motives:

  1. Fear of Punishment
  2. Anticipation of Reward
  3. Crude Conformity—Peer Pressure
  4. Majority Rules—Status Quo
  5. Self-Evident Truths—Natural Law
  6. Love and Truth Rule

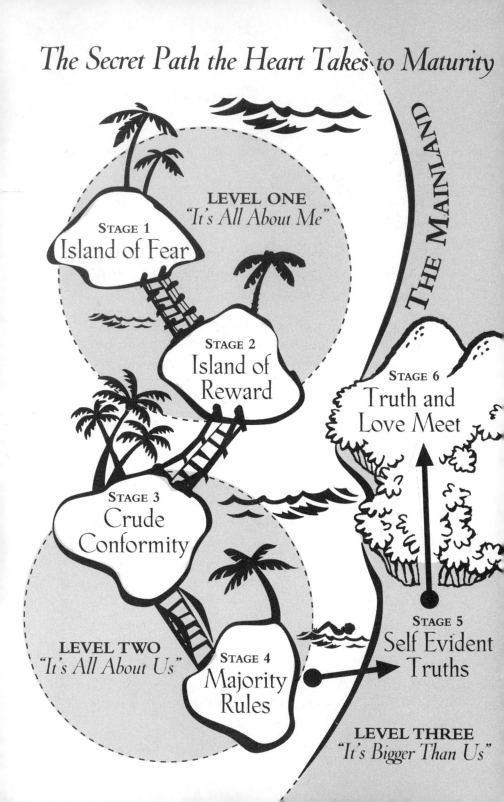

The Secret Path the Heart Takes to Maturity

THE MAINLAND

LEVEL ONE
"It's All About Me"

STAGE 1
Island of Fear

STAGE 2
Island of
Reward

STAGE 6
Truth and
Love Meet

STAGE 3
Crude
Conformity

STAGE 5
Self Evident
Truths

LEVEL TWO
"It's All About Us"

STAGE 4
Majority
Rules

LEVEL THREE
"It's Bigger Than Us"

CHAPTER 2

Stage One— The Island of Fear

"I'm afraid of pain, failure, or being out of control."

Fear of punishment is what motivates us on the first island of our journey.

I drive my car in this stage . . . I fear getting a ticket! I have had some experience with traffic tickets and I'd kind of like to avoid getting more experience. When a church I had worked for gave me a good-bye party, they had two people put on a skit. One wore a cardboard three-dimensional car that was made to look just like my car. Another person wore a cardboard police car. Suspenders held both cars on their shoulders. The skit was a reenactment of a ticket I had gotten once on my way to church. I drive a lot, so my risk for traffic tickets is high. (At least that's my story, and I'm sticking to it.) But after that skit I realized that I need to *morally develop* my driving habits. It had come to the point where I would see a patrol car and I'd panic even when I was going way under the speed limit (which does actually happen sometimes).

I determined that I needed to *up* the maturity level of my driving. I had to intentionally decide to change my inner motivations. So I talked to myself while driving down the road. "Aren't these other drivers precious people? I don't know them, but I know that God loves them. I must be careful as I drive so as to protect them and also to protect myself because God loves me too!" I am training myself to jump from Stage One driving to Stage Six driving. Since I have progressed through the stages and am capable of operating at Stage Six in other arenas, it is not impossible for me to make this change. But this is a deep change, so it may be a while before I arrive there.

The Importance of Stage One

God used this early stage of moral development with Adam and Eve in the garden. He told them not to eat the fruit of the Tree of the Knowledge of Good and Evil—or they would die. Like us, Adam and Eve were created as ever-maturing creatures, and God dealt with them in the way they would best understand.

Children are born into an entry-level position on the moral development scale. Look at their reflexes: The most prominent and dramatic reflex is the "startle" reflex in response to the baby's fear of falling. The entire body flails when this reflex is triggered.

Although we lose that specific reflex, we always keep certain basic survival instincts that are vital to a healthy life. In fact, because of this, a white layer of protective "insulation" protects the right side of the brain. The right side of the brain oversees all of the vital survival instincts—instincts that are rooted in *fear*. The left side (the gray side) does not have that protective layer. (Yes, your brain is two different colors because of this.) We are hard-wired to start life at Stage One.

The fear of punishment is a natural place to start on the journey to a mature heart. God's word exhorts us not to spare our children punishment for their wrongdoing, because in the world there is a direct link between wrongdoing and pain. Early on as a mother I realized how passionately I wanted my children to associate some sort of pain or unhappiness with disobedience and wrongdoing. And from the child's perspective, it is a wonderful thing to learn life's lessons in the safety of a loving home. How shortsighted for a parent to neglect the administration of punishment, leaving that child to be punished later by a very harsh and cruel world.

Please do not misunderstand. Children need love, nurture, and a lot of tenderness. But they also need to learn about the world. There is a balance that needs to be struck for good parenting to take place. I have seen some parents take delight in what they call "toughening up their child," while in reality they were just being cruel. I know that there are parents who have to be careful about *how* they discipline their children because of suffering abuse as a child.

But then there are people on the other end of the spectrum who wish to shelter their child from *every* microscopic particle of pain. There needs to be a balance. A good rule of thumb is to remember that a child's best interest for now and the future must always be at the forefront of any punishment.

The best punishments are those that help the child reason. Decision-making development hinges on making connections and discoveries about life. If the child doesn't play with others in a nice way, a good, reasonable punishment is a time-out from play. When a child is learning about the place of pain in life, which is what he is doing at Stage One, that pain needs to be connected to the offense.

Parents often think immediately of *physical* pain when they hear the word *pain*. But when I use the word, I mean pain the way a child sees it. Small children see time-outs as painful. (At least we can assume that since they cry loudly and kick up a fuss when we impose one.) Teenagers see restrictions on their freedom as painful. So we must be careful not to think too narrowly about "pain."

As a parent our goal at this stage is for our children to learn the important links between wrongdoing and pain within the loving environment of our homes. Zig Ziglar says, "The child who has not been disciplined with love by his little world will be disciplined generally without love by the big world."[1]

Fear is the crude beginning, the starting place from which children learn to deal with their world. God's word says in Psalm 11:10 that the fear of the Lord is the beginning of wisdom. Fearing the Lord is a good thing. It is the *beginning* of maturity. Stage One may be a crude beginning, but it is a beginning.

THE DOWNSIDE OF THIS STAGE

There is a dark side of Stage One. Children (and adults) who never progress further will either become bullies or "the bullied." Either they will wield their power by force or cower in fear. Some of you may have bosses who operate at this level! Do you know any people who manipulate those around them by their anger? They are operating out of Stage One decision making.

How about people who allow themselves to be manipulated by such a person? The people who are manipulated allow it mainly because they *fear the wrath* that will be unleashed on them if they won't comply. The resources of people operating at Stage One are so limited that they have to rely on crude power or cringing fear to function.

That is what Stage One is all about. It is our first resource out of which to make decisions. It is not a very sophisticated or mature stage. But it is definitely a starting place from which we can grow and mature to other stages of moral development.

Moving Beyond Stage One

As a parent you can help your children process and mature through the different stages. Each stage is like an island, connected to the next stage by a bridge. Parents with an intentional focus can help their children cross the bridge by using the *handrails* provided. When they cross over to the next stage, your children are on their way to greater moral and spiritual maturity.

HANDRAIL NUMBER ONE: GOOD BOUNDARIES

One of the handrails on the bridge leaving the Stage One island is *good boundaries*. Examples of good boundaries are consistent bedtimes, television restrictions, and play area parameters. These are your child's friend. Your children may not always appreciate them, but good boundaries are essential for creating a safe environment in which they can morally

mature. Surrounded with good boundaries, they can experience the safety they need to leave the Island of Fear.

When our children were ages five, six, and seven we had
a pool installed in our backyard. I dearly wanted our children
to love the water. However, I also wanted them to fear it. Two
of our children had drawn the conclusion that pool time was
just like bath time, except bigger and outside, so they loved
the water. Then we had one who disliked and mistrusted such
a large body of water imposing on his swing-set space. We
needed to instill a little respectful fear into the two water lovers and at the same time create an environment in which our
land lover could discover the joy of water. The solution for
both was . . . good boundaries! Our rules were simple:

1. No child in the pool without a parent in the pool area
2. Flotation devices required (while the children were young
   and inexperienced)
3. No dunking others
4. Only pool toys in the pool

The rules of the pool were diligently enforced so we could
create a safe place to play. The rules taught the water lovers
that there were dangers to avoid, but they also created a safe
place for the land lover to overcome his timidity of the water,
which he did in a very short time.

Parents face the dilemma of needing to instill the balance
of love and fear in their children in so many arenas of life. We
want our children to love people but fear strangers. We want
our children to enjoy play but fear exhaustion enough to go
to bed on time. We want them to enjoy eating but fear a
stomachache enough to develop an appetite for healthy food.
Good boundaries are the key to developing the delicate balance between love and fear. In fact, when good boundaries

are in place it allows fear to morph into a much healthier attitude—respect!

Good, healthy boundaries are an essential tool in your parenting tool belt. But don't be surprised by what a bad rap they get in modern culture. The culture is screaming, "We want freedom without boundaries! Freedom without boundaries is the only true freedom!" It's not true, of course, but people listen to those claims. Parents who listen tend to back off on setting good boundaries; some may even apologize for those they do set. This is detrimental to a child's development.

Good boundaries create the safety our children need to leave the Island of Fear. And oh, how we want and need to see this happen, because it is *dangerous* for children to get stuck at the lowest stages of development. Kohlberg's studies showed that people incarcerated in jails and prisons were most likely to test at the first two stages of development. This fact should compel us to vigorously work with our children toward heart maturity. Since boundaries are a part of propelling them forward, embracing good boundaries is an important part of the parenting plan. Boundaries are truly a wonderful gift to children.

Important Aspects of Good Boundaries

1. Good boundaries are rooted in relationship.

Josh McDowell says that rules without relationship leads to rebellion. In one of his books he shows it as an equation: Rules − Relationship = Rebellion.[2] Sometimes we get so hung up on the "rules" we forget that the "rules" are just one of God's ways of developing us for a healthier relationship with Him.

Don't you find it interesting that God *didn't* give Adam

and Eve the Ten Commandments (The Rules) at the edge of the Garden as He sent the couple out into the world? In fact, He waited thousands of years before he gave the world His rules. In those thousands of years He was developing relationships with people. Eventually, when He finally did give us the rules, He communicated clearly that we were not to give the rules to our children outside of the context of relationship (as we sit, walk, and stand with them). God is relationship oriented with us, and He wants us to be the same with our children.

This means our children need to sense that our relationship with them is our highest priority in the human realm. Many times, because we are more interested in their outward behavior, what we communicate to our children is that we only care about what they *do,* not who they *are.* To overcome this, we must work consistently to continue developing and enriching our relationships.

2. Good boundaries are more about freedom *than* restriction.

So why do we associate boundaries with restriction? *Surprise! This attitude is not restricted to kids.*

I love to ask parents, "What do you think about the Old Testament law 'an eye for an eye, a tooth for a tooth'?" Often they respond with words like *vindictive, mean,* or *hateful.* But it was God who gave the rule. Is He vindictive, mean, or hateful?

What was His reason for giving that rule?

Well, He gave that rule, and others like it, to a culture that was steeped in revenge. If someone was hurt in any way there were *no boundaries* on their quest for revenge. You may remember reading about Jacob's daughter, Dinah, in Genesis 34. She was raped by a man in a nearby town. Dinah's brothers went into that town and killed every male, and then they took all the women, children, and belongings as their spoils. So when God gave us the "eye for an eye" rule, He was actually *limiting* revenge for a culture that was not developmentally mature enough to understand grace yet.

When we look at things from a lower perspective in terms of spiritual development, boundaries *always* look negative and restricting. It is quite normal for children to see only the negative side of the boundaries parents set.

When I was a Montessori schoolteacher I once kept a gerbil in a cage in my classroom. Soon after I purchased the gerbil it escaped. I quickly caught it and put it back in the cage, but I soon realized that I needed to tape the top to the cage in order to prevent its escaping again. The gerbil, filled with hope that it could escape again, chewed faithfully on the tape every night. Why couldn't the gerbil be content to live in the beautiful cage filled with interesting things for him to do? Why did he continue to try to escape into a very dangerous world where he would surely starve to death, or worse? Finally the gerbil died. He had ingested too much tape and not enough food!

That's what boundaries are like with our children. Boundaries make up the "cage" that keeps them safe. Children can be like gerbils, ignoring the blessing of safety, thinking that if the walls of the cage were not there it would be so much *better* for them.

What children do not know is there is always a cat across the room, watching them chew on the restrictions. That cat is just hoping . . . hoping . . . hoping that they will succeed in escaping the boundaries. Your job as a parent is to know about the cats and to lovingly and consistently keep the boundaries intact, even while being misunderstood.

Children who are too young to understand about the "cats" in life will automatically assume that the boundary enforcers (you and I) are just being mean—trying to ruin their social life. Sometimes as loving parents we have to be willing to be misunderstood, just like God has been over the centuries. Through it all He continues to love, nurture, and seek relationship with us. He is unmistakably the perfect example for us as parents.

3. *Good boundaries are based on* values and expectations.

Good, solid reasons are vital for setting up good boundaries. Communicating that you do not want your child to do a particular thing because it will embarrass you is *not* a good reason. All boundaries need to be tethered to a value or an expectation. For example, we can say, "We expect a certain level of orderliness in our home, so please don't leave your backpack on the kitchen table after school." Another example: The reason you don't allow your child to take toys from or hit playmates is *not* that you don't want the playmates or their parents to get mad at you. Rather, it's because you as a family want to show how much you value other people and respect their property.

This becomes very important when dealing with teenagers. When they ask, *Are body piercings or tattoos evil?* your reasons need to be rooted in values and expectations. Otherwise they may be ignored because your teens see the reasons as unreasonable or ignorant. In our family, one of the reasons we say no to tattoos is because they are a *permanent* decision being made by a person who is *not fully grown*.

We feel it is unwise to let the seventeen-year-old garage-band leader make decisions for his *future self*—a twenty-eight-year-old executive. The value is on the seventeen-year-old's *future freedom*—that it not be limited by an immature decision. There are many angles to come from on this type of subject, but just declaring that tattoos or piercings are "evil" will not satisfy some strong-willed teenagers and will not teach them your values and expectations.

Parents of teenagers get weary of being tested by them. It seems that teens are constantly pushing the boundaries. I always counsel these parents to see those moments as opportunities—opportunities to teach values, not necessarily by lecture but through careful leading questions. *If I let you do what you want to do, how will that impact your future and where you want to go? How would that decision impact our family? What negative consequences might you have to bear? Is it worth it? Who else could potentially be hurt by your actions?* These kinds of questions show what you value and protect.

Good boundaries—based on values and expectations, and a strong relationship with our child—are the first handrail on the bridge that leaves the Stage One Island of Fear. The second handrail is about boundaries as well, but it is such a distinctively vital part of boundaries that it becomes handrail number two.

HANDRAIL NUMBER TWO: CONSISTENT CONSEQUENCES

The second and most vital way to help a child get off the island of fear is to administer consistent consequences. Setting good boundaries is only half of the program. Parents need to be diligent and consistent in *enforcing* the boundaries.

The motivation behind being consistent should *not* be behavior control. You will be much more determined and inspired to be consistent if you remember you are actually helping your child mature by being so diligent. I find that parents who are interested only in behavior control tend to be random in administering consequences. Often they enforce the boundaries only when the behavior disrupts or bothers them.

The Power of Hope

Being consistent in consequences is all about a powerful force called *hope*. The power of hope in a person's life is incredible. It is the force that keeps people alive and sane in concentration camps. And hope is a potent force you can use to help your child mature.

When a parent uses consistent consequences, the child is kept from *growing the hope* that he or she can get away with bad behavior. On the other hand, random consequences can actually *feed* the hope that they can get away with bad behavior. Because of this, studies have actually shown that no consequences are more effective than random consequences.

My husband and I learned this the hard way. We had the totally misguided notion that the end goal of assigning weekly chores to our children was so that we could maintain a more orderly house with less effort. All you experienced parents can stop laughing now! Really, you could damage your lungs laughing that hard.

We put the chore plan together as a family. We posted the chores on the refrigerator. We talked about the chores at family meetings. The only thing we did not do was administer *consistent consequences* for undone chores. We just kept struggling every day . . . reminding, reminding, randomly administering consequences, and many times eventually doing the chores ourselves. When I admit this in front of any given group of parents, I am amazed at how many identify with our failure.

Once we finally figured out our mistake it was too late; the word *chores* had been permanently deactivated in all of our vocabularies. So we started a new program of chores under a new name: *Responsibilities*. Under the new program, my husband and I learned not to assign any responsibilities unless we were prepared to follow up by visually confirming that the responsibility had been done and then administering consequences if it had not. Consistency is the key to success with any boundary.

THE TWO HANDRAILS TOGETHER

Good boundaries and consistent consequences together create a stable, safe environment for our children to explore the idea of a higher motive than fear.

I struggled when I first began to develop this material because fear was such a negative place to start. The first two handrails, boundaries and consequences, seemed like a negative way to start a parenting plan. But the truth is that fear of pain is a very powerful motivator.

The *fear* of pain is actually a *greater* motivator than the actual pain itself! In times of war or espionage the *fear of pain* is used to extract information from the enemy. Those who are bound by law not to use actual pain can still quite successfully use the fear of pain as a motivator because this is how we are wired as human beings. The greatest, most primal instinct we have is our survival instinct, which is activated by fear.

Good parents don't *cause* their child's fear. They simply deal with the reality of their fear, primarily by creating a safe environment for their children. Since there is no way to create a "pain-free" environment, they need to create an environment that has safe places marked by boundaries—where pain can be successfully avoided by the choices that the child makes. This is a great gift to a child. It puts a lot of power into his or her hands—the power to avoid what humans fear most: pain.

Here is how the two handrails work together:

1. Set Boundary
2. Communicate Boundary
3. Boundary Tested (Don't be surprised! This is on their to-do list!)
4. Consequences Administered
5. Child Expresses Anger or Sadness (This is also on their to-do list!)
6. Parent Stays Lovingly Firm
7. Child Accepts Boundary
8. Important: May repeat Steps 3–6 *several times* before reaching Step 7

This is a simple and somewhat obvious list, but it is important to be aware that boundaries *will be tested*.

Number eight serves as a reminder to us that setting and enforcing boundaries is a process with a built-in "loop." Like many of the new choruses we sing at church, the process may loop many, many, many times before reaching the ending note. If a parent caves in on being consistent, the song ends without ever reaching the sweet "amen."

It is also important to be prepared for your child's expressions of sadness or anger. It's good at this point to remind yourself that *you are not responsible for your child's happiness.* You are, however, responsible for their safety, health, spiritual and mental education, and growth toward moral maturity.

By their very nature boundaries seem to make children angry or sad. It's important for you to remember that good, consistent boundaries reflecting your expectations and values will help your child's decision-making process mature. A loving parent who *expects* some sadness and anger can respond lovingly without being manipulated by their emotion.

I have had parents ask, "How do you accept and deal with the anger a child displays regarding a boundary and be sure that you are not 'exasperating' him as the Bible admonishes us not to do?" (Ephesians 6:4).

This Scripture highlights why it is so important that parents carefully establish boundaries that reflect their values and expectations. It puts the boundaries at a higher level than just personal preference. But, even with careful thought, parents have been known to be wrong. So it's important to establish a way for your children to *respectfully* question a boundary. Give them the words to use, such as: "Can I respectfully question this boundary?"

When this happens, make sure you listen carefully, like a loving judge. After listening, ask yourself: *Does he have a valid point? Are there changes I could make in the boundary that would meet all of our needs better? Or is he (or she) simply manipulating me, or being argumentative?* This simple addition to the system can keep communication open between parents and children in places where bitterness might otherwise creep in.

Another important factor to consider is that *bitterness implies the passing of time.* Children may initially express sadness or anger regarding a boundary, but most come to accept and respect it within a fairly short period of time. Bitterness sets in when anger has been allowed to ferment and fester over a long period of time. To make sure this doesn't happen we need to foster our parent/child *relationship* and keep it strong and healthy. Parents will be so much less likely to embitter their children if they are listening and spending the time necessary to develop and maintain a good relationship with them.

So . . . boundaries with consistent consequences—how simple! In fact, it may be too simple for some. You may already know and practice all you have read so far. I encourage you to keep reading. This is a process, and the earlier steps in the process are widely known and practiced. There are many books you can read about parenting boundaries. However, as we get closer to the goal (the Mainland), the process is far less commonly known and practiced. Please read on!

Summary: Chapter Two

The primary motive in Stage One is fear. The person operating at Stage One is afraid of punishment (pain, failure, or being out of control).

The important concept learned at Stage One:
Staying inside the boundaries (having respect for the boundaries) is more secure!

Handrails parents can use to help their child get off the Stage One island:
1. Good Boundaries
   Remember, good boundaries are:

   • Rooted in Relationship

   • More about Freedom than Restriction

   • Based on Values and Expectations

2. Consistent Consequences
   Remember, inconsistent consequences for poor choices feed your child's hope that he or she can disrespect boundaries without consequences.

Footnotes:
1. Zig Ziglar, *Raising Positive Kids in a Negative World* (Nashville, TN: Thomas Nelson, 1985), 210.
2. Josh McDowell, *The Disconnected Generation* (Nashville, TN: Word Publishing, 2000), 28.

CHAPTER 3

Stage Two— The Island of Reward

"What's in it for me?"

Stage Two is the *Anticipation of Reward*. This is the stage I operate at when I decide to get the mail.

My husband and I are opposites. I've heard that most couples are. I can't wait to get the mail every day because "there might be a surprise card, or a letter from a dear friend, or even some unexpected money!" My husband, who's all hung up on reality, reminds me that far more bills come in the mail on a regular basis than cards or money. But I hang on to my hope and retrieve the mail at the first available opportunity.

When I travel out of town without my husband I am stunned when I call him at eight or nine o'clock in the evening and he hasn't even thought of the mail! I can't understand that at all. Is he not remotely curious as to what secret reward may be lying in that little box? He has learned to defend himself by sweetly saying that he can't help himself; he makes the decision to get the mail in "Stage One—fear of bills."

How Stage Two Works

Stage Two is a place where decisions are made according to what will most likely bring comfort or pleasure to the decision maker. Children can often be found on the Stage Two island. Think of the toddler who wants what he *wants*. If it's good or pleasurable in any way, he wants it right now! It reminds me of a joke my dad sent to me a while back. It's called—

The Property Laws of a Toddler

If I like it, it's mine.
If it's in my hand, it's mine.
If I can take it from you, it's mine.
If I had it a little while ago, it's mine.
If it's mine, it must not appear to be yours in any way.
If I'm building something, *all* the pieces are mine.
If it looks like mine, it *is* mine.
If I saw it first, it's mine.
If you are playing with something and you put it down, it
    automatically becomes mine.
If it's broken . . .
. . . it's yours!

Stage Two is where people (adults or children) merely seek what *they want*—whatever it takes to satisfy their personal needs or wants. Eve committed the first sin at this stage. She saw that the forbidden fruit was desirable. And suddenly the fear of punishment was overridden by her anticipation of something desirable. This is how the world works for us as well. The lower stages of decision making do not serve us effectively. Over time, circumstances have a way of uncovering the flaws in them.

Stage Two is an important building block for maturity. Realizing there are certain actions that will bring about desired results allows us to become *self-motivated* individuals. God doesn't want us to ignore the blessings that come as a result of following His laws; in fact, throughout the Bible He promises certain blessings or benefits as a result of our obedient actions and attitudes.

It is critical for children to associate good decisions with rewards. In this broken world we adults know that good decisions are not *always* rewarded, but this principle is still an important developmental link for a child. Once established, this link will not easily break down when they later find out it's not guaranteed to work for them every time. As they grow up they begin to realize that their good decisions may not always be rewarded immediately either. In fact, sometimes they may even be punished in the beginning. For example, cutting corners and cheating can seemingly produce instant results, while honesty and integrity may not pay off for years.

THE DOWNSIDE OF STAGE TWO

The downside of Stage Two is that people who make the majority of their decisions at the reward stage are saying that whatever they desire is *right* for them. Sounds like a pretty hedonistic way to live. If everyone were to live at this stage, the world would be a dangerous place because a lot of sin is committed at Stage Two. Think of the sins spoken of in the Commandments, like covetousness, stealing, and murder. The person who commits these sins is doing what he or she wants without any regard for the rights of others. If everyone acted at Stage Two it would be like the earth was filled with two-year-olds!

We've all seen small children happily make themselves at home at this stage—like when their "blankee" is left at Aunt Lynda's house, and regardless of what time of night it is or what time everyone has to get up the next morning, their "blankee" must be retrieved *that night*! In fact, the child may even be upset and not understand why it takes so long to drive back to Aunt Lynda's house. All that matters to them is their own immediate desire being satisfied.

Moving Beyond Stage Two

In order for a child to move beyond Stage Two there are some important connections that must be made. First, there must be a basic foundation of nurture and care established for them. They also must know the difference between a reward and a met need. Although rewards can be *random*, basic care must be *consistent*. Otherwise, the result is the same as not having boundaries: chaos! When basic physical, mental, spiritual, and emotional needs are not met, it creates internal chaos in children, and we all know learning can't take place in chaos. So it makes sense that the first handrail on the bridge taking us off of this island deals with a nurturing foundation.

HANDRAIL NUMBER ONE:
PROACTIVE AND SUPPORTIVE CARE

Growing children have many needs. They need attention, affection, and admiration—just to name a few. Part of helping our children leave the Stage Two island is to provide an environment in which their real physical and emotional needs are consistently met. In the same way that children are much less likely to learn on an empty stomach, unmet needs can keep them from making the important link between good decisions and rewards.

The first handrail on the bridge leading off of the Island of Reward has two elements to it: Proactive and Supportive Care.

Proactive Care

This is when a parent *looks for opportunities* to meet his or her child's needs. As proactive parents, we will actively work with our children to help them solve their current problems— whether it means putting child locks on the lower cabinets when children are small to keep them safe from dangerous substances, or helping them to research colleges and careers as they plan their future lives. We shouldn't regularly do for our children what they can do for themselves, but we *should* offer help in ever-changing ways as our children mature.

Supportive Care

The other half of the care a child needs from his parents is supportive care. While proactive care is about teaching and providing, supportive care is more emotional. Emotional needs are as important to address as the physical and instructional needs of our kids. Meeting both needs could look like this:

Your child falls and hurts her arm:

- Proactive: You treat the hurt arm or take her to the doctor to make sure her physical needs are adequately met.

- Supportive: You ask her how much it hurts; empathize with and comfort her.

In another case, your child is the only one in his class who was not invited to a party, and he expresses disappointment about it to you:

- Proactive: You help him formulate an alternative plan for that day.

- Supportive: You let him talk about his hurt feelings without dismissing them. Then you comfort him, maybe by telling about a time when the same thing happened to you and how sad you felt about it.

Maybe your child is having trouble with math. Here's how the two kinds of care would look:

- Proactive: You help her with her math problems in the evening (if you understand them), or you find a tutor who can help her.

- Supportive: You acknowledge her frustration and assure her that it's quite normal to be successful in some subjects and struggle in others.

Proactive care is the antiseptic and the Band-Aid.
Supportive care is the kiss of comfort.

It's important to deal with your children's emotions gently, whether they are sadness, frustration, fear, or anger. Emotions themselves are not evil. The acts behind the emotions can be, but emotions are just responses to what has happened, and none of us can dictate what form our emotions will take. Whatever emotion your child brings to you should be validated, soothed, and then treated with both proactive and supportive care.

If you discount your child's emotions with statements like "don't be angry" or "don't be sad," you won't *change* her emotion. You will simply communicate to her that you don't want her to share what is on her heart with you. Remember, the fastest way to alienate your child from you is to *discount his or her emotional responses.*

In fact, a good parenting principle to keep in mind is this: If your child comes to you in an emotional state about something, respond with *emotion*, not facts or instruction. Match emotionally expressed needs with emotion (empathetic soothing).

Am I saying that you should validate the "monster in the closet" or your child's untrue perceptions? No. But when they are expressing emotion, try to figure out what the *deeper* emotional need is. In the case of the monster in the closet, deal with your child's sense of insecurity. My husband and I found that after we had taken the time to soothe our children, it was much more effective to talk about the fact that "Jesus can watch over you and protect you as you sleep, no matter what," rather than opening up their closet every night for "monster inspections."

At certain developmental stages a child's brain is developing rapidly in some areas and slowly in others. In early adolescence their brains may be working overtime in the part that deals with raw emotion, while the part of the brain that deals with logic is almost in hibernation. Those of you with teenagers are probably relieved to hear that explanation. *No wonder my teenager has been reacting that way! My logical lectures are being received like I'm speaking Greek!* If the raging fire of raw emotion can be soothed *first,* the logical help that follows will be much more effective.

HANDRAIL NUMBER TWO: RANDOM REWARDS

Another way to help your child mature beyond Stage Two is to practice giving *random rewards.* The practice of random rewards is much like using consistent consequences (a handrail from the Island of Fear), but one is negative in its effect and the other is positive. Consistent consequences *starve* the hope that a child can "get away with" his poor choices, while random rewards *feed* the good hope that "I will receive a reward because of my good decisions." Practiced together, these two handrails can be highly effective in helping our children mature in their moral development.

I believe that hope is the most powerful force a parent can nurture in a child—as long as the hope is placed in what is secure. Be sure to stir hope toward the right goal; otherwise you risk unleashing a powerful force that can propel your child in the opposite direction you had intended! To anchor their hope in what will eventually disappoint them is to create the kind of hope that Proverbs talks about. "Hope deferred makes the heart sick, but a longing fulfilled is a tree of life" (Proverbs 13:12). Promising rewards that you don't follow through on, or using rewards to *control behavior* rather than *mature your children,* will not produce good hope in their hearts.

How to "Grow" Hope

Using random rewards builds incredible hope in a child because they feed the hope that *good decisions* will produce

good rewards. Surprisingly, consistent rewards are not n
effective as random ones.

Why would that be true? Because hope is grown in a *vac-uum.* Paul wrote, "Hope that is seen is no hope at all. Who hopes for what he already has? But if we hope for what we do not yet have, we wait for it patiently" (Romans 8:24–25). The *random* part of the reward technique is what makes it so vital. It is not in the giving of rewards but in the *waiting* between rewards that hope flourishes in a heart.

I once observed a young mother who was trying to moti-vate her preschool sons to behave by offering them a reward. She had a bag of goodies—candy and small toys—that was kept up on the top of the refrigerator. Once a day the reward bag was brought down, usually after they had napped, as con-sistent in the boys' schedule as their naptime. She told them what she expected of them in terms of behavior and warned them that if they did not meet those expectations they would not receive their after-nap reward.

To my surprise, the threat of missing the reward seemed to have absolutely no effect on her children's behavior. At first I thought maybe they were not motivated because the promised reward was to be received *later,* and the children were too young to be motivated for something so far into the future. However, as I continued to observe this mother, I noticed that her negotiation didn't work in either case—whether it was before their nap or after it. I just couldn't figure out why the children weren't motivated by the goodies.

Finally I realized the reason: The reward was too consis-tent. It had become "cheap" in the boys' eyes. The promise of reward was not building any hope in them because it was too predictable; there was no "vacuum" element.

It's better if parents plan to randomly "catch" their

children doing good things and *then* reward that behavior or character trait. I used to get silver or gold certificate stickers and write the word *Commendation* on them. My children were ridiculously too young to even know what the word *commendation* meant, but every once in a while—when I would randomly catch one of them doing something that was good, without my involvement in their decision—I would issue them a "Medal of Commendation."

At first I did it because I saw a behavior I wanted to reward and I had nothing fitting in the house except a funny gold sticker. I think it came with a *Reader's Digest* sweepstakes application. But the action was so well received that I made it part of my reward plan. Today my teenagers still remember receiving their "medals" with pride. And when I laugh about it they look at me with disapproval. It was serious business to them!

When choosing a reward, some criteria you might want to shoot for are:

- Keying in to your child's interest(s)

- Generating the "rare and valuable" element by creating scarcity

- Employing the element of surprise

Keying in to your child's interest is crucial to motivating your child. When I was a teenager my dad very effectively keyed in to my interest in musical instruments. The more I focused on my instruments and filled the house with music, the more he indulged my interest. He researched the weirdest instruments ever made and shared his findings with me.

I remember to this day one particular family treat night—having dinner at a pizza parlor that featured a huge pipe organ. The restaurant was selected because the organ was an instrument I enjoyed playing, and my father knew it would interest me. I also loved the marimba, so another time my father researched the idea of building one for me, but in the end he found a nice used one that he purchased for me.

And now I'm reciprocating. A few weeks ago I heard about a marimba concert that was going to be held at a local church. I asked my dad if I could kidnap him for the night and take him to a special event (not telling him what I had planned). As the event drew nearer I couldn't wait to see my dad's face when he realized it was a marimba concert! In one of my moments of anticipation, however, a random thought surfaced that set my bliss back a bit. I wondered, *What if my dad had only been "keying in to my interest"—and doesn't have any personal interest in marimbas at all?* Fortunately, all my worries were dispelled the night of the event. I could tell that he *loved* the concert. Maybe he had keyed in to my interest so effectively for all those years that it became his own!

Keying in to your child's interest for the purpose of reward giving accomplishes two things. First, it enhances the effectiveness of the reward. Not only does the reward come with an "'atta-boy" or "'atta-girl," but it also is valuable in and of itself to the child. Secondly, keying in to your child's interest is an indirect way to show that you appreciate him or her as a distinct and unique person in the family!

Scarcity is the main element for creating a "rare and valuable" feel for the reward. You can create scarcity by being careful to give just the right amount of a reward. Remember, a small morsel is a more memorable reward than a huge portion. Once I bought a large plastic bag of glow-in-the-dark ants. They were small, about the size of a larger-sized real ant. If I had given the bag full of ants to my children as one reward, all at once, they would have regarded them as virtually valueless in a very short period of time. Instead, I gave them one . . . at . . . a . . . time. I called them the "Ant Award."

This is how I would create the rare and valuable element in their minds. I'd say something like, "Hey, did you know that an ant is able to carry up to ten times its weight? Isn't that remarkable? Well, I think what you did just now was also remarkable, so I am awarding you the 'Ant Award.'"

Another great element for maximizing reward giving is the element of surprise. The reward itself should be a surprise—don't promise it up front, ahead of time. That changes the nature of the reward. It becomes more of a negotiated benefit, like different amounts of money promised for different letter grades in school. Those kinds of negotiations are fine, especially if they work for you. But those kinds of situations don't build hope in a child the way random surprise rewards can.

The element of surprise helps create the anticipatory vacuum that allows hope to grow so well. The reward itself can also be really surprising. The ants in themselves were not all that exciting to my children at first—until they realized that the ants glowed in the dark, and they could stick them to the wall near their bed and "collect 'em."

Here's one warning that I would give regarding rewards: Try not to give expensive rewards. It will be a test of your creativity to do this, but it is so important that the " 'atta-kid" enthusiasm not get lost in a huge gift. Rewards are not at all about material value. They are about *communicating admiration* for the character and maturity you are beginning to see in your child. They are about showing your children that you've paid attention to their interests.

I think in our culture we need to be careful not to overindulge and therefore attach too much value to material things. Sometimes it can also show our own insecurity about the affection of our children. We feel that we have to buy something big to impress them and keep them "on our side." But families that are secure in their mutual love don't have to impress one another with expensive material things.

CHECK YOUR OWN MOTIVES

The handrails on the bridge leading off of the Island of Reward may be tools that you are already using in parenting. If so, I encourage you to continue to use them! You may be able to tweak them and be much more effective if you check *your* motives from time to time. Ask yourself some questions like, *Am I giving proactive and supportive care to create a loving, safe environment for my child, or do I just hope to bypass bigger hassles or louder crying by using them? Do I practice random rewards only because I'm too distracted with life to be consistent? Do I reward my children only when I'm feeling "parent-guilt"?*

As we wrestle to discover our children's motives it is good to remember that our children have a much easier time discovering ours than we do discovering theirs! I don't know why this is true, and I certainly agree that it is not fair. But those are the cards we are dealt. If you are just trying to keep your house clean and the noise level down, or trying to keep up with the neighbors, or trying to ease some guilt you've accumulated, your children will quite easily discern your real motivation.

If, however, you are using these principles as part of your desire to fulfill God's plan for your family—to develop children with mature hearts toward God and His word—your kids will likely know that as well. If our hearts are right, and we use the principles discussed with greater consistency and loving determination, we can expect some tremendous spiritual and moral growth in every member of the family (including ourselves).

Summary: Chapter Three

The primary motive at Stage Two is the anticipation of reward. The heart at this low level of development is thinking, *What's in it for me?*

The important concept to be discovered at Stage Two:
The direct link between good decisions and rewards (certain actions will bring about favorable results).

Handrails for getting off the Stage Two island:

1. Proactive and Supportive Care:

- Proactive care is when parents look for ways to meet or help meet their children's physical (presented) needs.

- Supportive care is vital emotional support that meets their unseen emotional needs.

Remember, *both* are necessary in nurturing your children.

2. Random Rewards
Remember, random rewards feed *good* hope in your children!

Three important elements of Random Rewards:

- Keying in to your child's interest(s)

- Generating the "rare and valuable" element by creating scarcity

- Employing the element of surprise

CHAPTER 4

Level One—
It's All About Me!

Stages One and Two are like two islands grouped together that make up Level One in our development. The binding factor between the two islands is that all decisions are based solely on a person's fears and desires. Other people and their concerns or needs are *not* taken into account. In other words, for the person stuck between those two islands, "It's all about me!"

This is the place (ideally) where babies and small children learn about themselves and how to interact with the world around them. They learn the basic concepts of cause and effect. It's in this level that they receive the fabric necessary to sew themselves into self-motivated persons.

Level One is the place where parents can most effectively use the classic motivators—punishment and reward. The child's desire to avoid punishment and receive rewards is a good place to start in forming moral decisions. Reward and punishment are great motivators, but parents should be sure to use them to help develop mature hearts in their kids, not just to get them to "do" the right behavior when grown-ups are looking!

I shared the ideas from the "Secret Path the Heart Takes to Maturity" with a woman who works in the juvenile justice system in the town where I live. She became very excited learning about this phase because she realized that virtually all of the youth at her facility were operating most of the time at Level One in terms of their moral maturity. She suddenly realized that if those young people could be encouraged and compelled to mature to at least Stage Three, they would not be so likely to commit antisocial and unlawful acts. She was exactly right. Kohlberg's studies showed that most incarcerated prisoners are stuck on the twin islands of Stage One (fear of punishment) and Stage Two (anticipation of reward).

"It's All About Me" is a great place to visit and learn from, but if a person stays there permanently it becomes a tragedy. Young people need to be constantly challenged to grow toward a higher level of decision making. But because of the low expectations we have for them, we often simply smile and shake our heads at teenagers who are indulging in immature and selfish behavior.

There is a very rare degenerative brain disorder that is usually not detected at birth. In fact, this condition is so rare doctors do not have a name for it. The new baby will appear to be a perfect, healthy newborn. But throughout the first year, as unhealthy signs begin to appear, the disorder becomes alarmingly apparent and the bewildered parents must be told their baby will *never* mature. They are told that their sweet little child will always be an infant, both mentally and physically. What an incomprehensible heartbreak!

For as beautiful and sweet as a newborn is, no parent

wants to see his child *stay* a newborn. In fact, when it does, the sight of it becomes a portrait of an unspeakable tragedy— not hope and promise. That is the perspective we must have when we see immaturity in the hearts of our children. It has its place in their lives, but we want them to grow and mature as God intended.

So many times we are tempted to wink at our teenagers' immaturity, thinking, *They're just being teenagers!* I'm not suggesting we expect adult behavior from them; I just hope we can see immaturity for what it is—a destructive trend that needs to be carefully monitored. If maturity is to increase in our children, we need to see a corresponding decrease in their immaturity level. Antisocial behavior exhibited by our teens shouldn't be encouraged through indulgence. If we view irresponsibility, unresponsiveness to others, and disrespect of people and property as "cute" in our teenagers, we can expect them to act accordingly.

Moving Beyond the First Two Islands

We all start out as immature children, learning about ourselves, beginning our developmental journey in a broken world; it's easy to get stuck with *myself* as the center of our own universe. In time, however, what was to have been a beneficial stage, a sweet beginning, can become the noose around our neck if we're not careful.

As an educator I am passionate about moving students beyond the "It's All About Me" islands. Why so passionate? Because it's a dangerous area for teenagers these days. There are so many voices whispering to them: "Try me, you'll like me!" "I'll make you beautiful." "I'll keep you safe." "This will give you power." All of these voices are enticing siren songs to those who are considering only themselves in their decisions.

A lot of parents focus on motivating their teens not to do things like take drugs or engage in premarital sex strictly at the punishment/reward level. Teens are warned of the very real consequences they will suffer from such risky behavior. They are also appealed to on the basis of the very real rewards they will receive from making the right choices. While these positions are accurate and important, they still fall short because *they do not advance the teen's own reasoning skills.*

The reason that the "It's All About Me" islands are such a bad place to be stuck is that the reasoning skills required for making decisions here are very crude and ineffective in the long run. It's so easy to make poor decisions or have good decisions countered. For example, a girl is told in health class that she needs to be careful when having sex because she could become pregnant or contract a disease (fear of punishment). Those negative threats or natural consequences may motivate her to commit herself to abstinence for a time. But all her boyfriend has to do is show her the latest medical developments and make her feel safe from the harmful effects (or punishments) of premarital sex to counter this decision. By keeping our entire curriculum at Level One, without drawing students to a higher level of reasoning, we are not giving students the effective tools they need to *consistently make better moral decisions.*

Summary: Chapter Four

Stages One and Two are twin islands that use the "It's All About Me" mentality for making decisions. Together they make up Level One in our moral development.

- Stage One—Fear of Punishment

- Stage Two—Anticipation of Reward

The common denominator in these two stages is that it's all about *me*! Decisions are based on what I'm afraid of or what reward I want.

Remember: Although there are important concepts to be learned at Stages One and Two (as discussed in chapters two and three), Level One is a dangerous and antisocial place to be developmentally stuck, both for us and for our kids!

CHAPTER 5

Stage Three—The Island of Crude Conformity

"I want to be accepted."

When I was young and energetic I taught small children in a Montessori school. It was interesting to watch the children interact with their parents and their peers as they came to class each day.

One day I witnessed a familiar scene that made me curious. A mother was bringing her child to class late, and from across the parking lot it was obvious to me that they were both having a bad day. The child was having a mobile tantrum as the mother escorted her from the car to the classroom entryway. The little girl was fully absorbed in her Academy Award–winning performance until she realized that she was inside the classroom door and in the presence of her peers. Then a funny thing happened. The storm stopped in mid-thunder. She looked shyly around, obviously hoping she had not been caught "acting like a baby," and she sweetly glided to the circle and sat with her friends. I'd seen that happen many times before, but this time it made me wonder. What caused the little girl to stop so suddenly? She had thrown tantrums in front of her classmates earlier in the year. What had changed?

As I thought about it, I realized that she was developing socially. She was opening up her mind to the possibility that maybe she was not quite the center of the world. There were other people to be considered, and *what would they think of her?*

This child was having her first experience with Stage Three: Crude Conformity.

What's Different About This Stage?

At Stage Three we are making decisions based on a need to *belong* or *be accepted*. We suddenly begin to realize the importance of others in our lives. Now, this is admittedly just a short step from the "It's All About Me" islands, because we're not recognizing the importance of others for *their sake* but rather for *our sake*. But it is a step in the right direction to want to be accepted and to belong.

When our children enter this phase we have a term for what we commonly see. We call it peer pressure. But it isn't restricted to teenagers or children in early adolescence. As seen in the illustration above, it can start at a young age, and there are even some adults who don't mature beyond Stage Three. So living with peer pressure cuts across almost all ages.

If their peers are a good influence, then behavior will likely be good for the persons affected. But if their peers pressure them to exhibit bad behavior, they will have few resources to keep them from caving in and behaving badly.

Peer pressure in and of itself won't determine our behavior; it can cause us to make good decisions as well as bad ones. The apostle Paul challenged the Corinthians (who were living in a very morally immature culture) with these words: "Do not be misled: 'Bad company corrupts good character'" (1 Corinthians 15:33). Never more than at Stage Three are we vulnerable in regard to our choice of companions.

The Crude Conformity stage is, just like the preceding stage, a good place to travel through. It has its important lessons. However, to pitch a tent and *stay there* is far short of the destination we were designed to reach. So no matter what great and grand deeds a person does, if they are motivated only by the desire to be accepted, they are not yet mature.

THE IMPORTANCE OF THIS STAGE

The world gets larger for those who round the bend into the world of Stage Three. In Stages One and Two the individual was in a world in which *all that mattered* was the immediate needs of the "self." For obvious reasons it's good when we—and our children—can develop socially to the point that:

- We recognize other people exist, and

- We recognize they have opinions, needs, and desires that may be different from ours.

Have you ever been in a relationship that's all take and no give? If you're constantly on the giving end it can get old really quickly, even if you're a saint. I'm not talking about caring for someone who is weak and needs your care without being *able* to return your kindness. I'm talking about those people who *mine* others. They extract what they can from other people with no concern for equality in the relationship.

Healthy relationships need a balance of give and take. Some call this balance "quid pro quo." It is a healthy exchange of give and take between people, and is especially important in fostering healthy marriages and friendships.

Don't get me wrong. Stage Three is not a huge leap from Stage Two. Here we are *just beginning* to open our world to the consideration of others. It may only be a tiny step forward, but it is an important one. Other people are considered in our decisions mostly in relation to our needs, but at least they are given some consideration. We begin to wonder: *Do others like and accept me?*

THE DOWNSIDE OF STAGE THREE

The need to belong is powerful. If a child's family does not provide a safe place to belong and be accepted, then the child will probably work hard at getting that basic need met somewhere else. Children who need to go outside of their own family for acceptance are put at greater risk for being sexually abused or becoming involved with a group that promotes deviant behavior. These groups (like gangs, for instance) provide a place to belong, but they come at a high price. Moral development is way down on the list of priorities for most of these groups!

Parents can help safeguard their children from the drawbacks of Stage Three by making sure that each child's need for acceptance and approval is being met as much as possible. A human being's need for acceptance and approval is remarkably great, and those needs really begin to make themselves known at this stage. Parents can have a lot of influence in helping to develop and shape their children if they *recognize and meet their need to belong sufficiently.*

Meeting Their Needs for Acceptance

A couple of essential truths need to be learned at Stage Three. They are:

- A person's value does not change—regardless of behavior or circumstances

- Everyone needs grace (yes, even parents!)

How do we know our value does not change regardless of our behavior or circumstances? The value of all human beings is based on how much God paid for their redemption. In any economy, that's an unfathomable value. We also know that our behavior does not affect that value due to the fact that God paid the price while we were still sinners (Romans 5:6–8). It is important to understand this theological fact and *live it out* in how we interact with our children when they fall short of our expectations.

Think of how you sound when you are disciplining your child. Do you communicate that her bad behavior has changed her value to you in any way? Comments like "You are such a brat!" communicate that her behavior determines who she is. Any degrading "you are" statements infer that the child's value is changeable, depending on her behavior.

Communicating a child's permanent value and showing unconditional love will enable your children to find the acceptance they so desperately need at this stage of development, and to move on. How to communicate to them that they have unchanging value is the focus of the rest of this chapter.

HANDRAIL NUMBER ONE: PRAISE THEIR CHARACTER

One way to meet a child's need for acceptance in a very practical way is to praise his or her character rather than behavior. Sometimes busy parents remember to discipline but forget to affirm their children. It's important that our affirmations not rest solely on their good behavior in order for our kids to truly feel accepted and approved. Parents must let their children know they are valued *even when their behavior is wrong!* And when their behavior is good, it is much more powerful to see it (and praise it) as the *result* of their character, which flows from the heart.

Praising character rather than behavior is the difference between:

- Congratulating your child because he is so consistent in doing his chores (behavior) as opposed to admiring him for being *a diligent person* (character).

- Thanking your child for getting along so well with others on a family outing rather than marveling out loud to him about what *a caring and considerate person he is.*

- Thanking your child for waiting while you ran an errand or praising her for being such *a patient person.*

The difference in the words may be subtle, but the results are not! When we praise who our children are, rather than just how they perform, they feel approved at a much deeper level. When behavior is constantly praised, they may feel they are under pressure to continue to exhibit good behavior, because if they don't, the tide of approval may shift away from them. Inner character is the very essence of who we are, and we long for those we care about to see our "best part" and value us for that reason alone.

Almost any parent knows not to send messages that say, "You are a bad child." It can be so damaging over time if adults continually say things like "you *are* lazy, mean, selfish, a brat," etc. That's very different from telling our children that what they *did* (the deed) is naughty and should not be repeated or that they did not make a good decision.

Praising character is the same idea, only inverted. Praising the inner qualities of your child communicates that you are *looking* to see your child's best self. Most children think parents are only looking to catch their bad behavior! Praising character is a powerful and intentional way of showing your children that it is not that you just expect good behavior, but you see their good behavior as a reflection of who they really are (or could be) deep down inside.

One mom contacted me after attending one of my conferences, where I had shared the importance of praising character. She realized she was constantly praising her ten-year-old daughter for her outward behavior, and as a result the daughter was performance driven. She excelled in all the outward behaviors parents love—she cleaned her room, helped out around the house, and needed very little oversight. That set the mother up to praise her outward behavior on a regular basis, which propelled the daughter to strive even harder at performing.

Fortunately, the mother was inspired to change tactics with her daughter and committed herself to praising her character rather than her specific deeds. She started by going into her daughter's room to tuck her in. She had carefully compiled a list in her head of all the character traits she saw in her daughter and began to lay out for her daughter what she saw in her—things like diligence, resourcefulness, and initiative. To the mother's surprise, the daughter curled up into a fetal position and began to cry in response to the praise. A little alarmed, her mom asked, "Honey, why are you crying?" The daughter replied, "Because it feels so good!" Praising character touches a deep place in the soul of your child because it so eloquently communicates unreserved acceptance.

The following is a list of some character traits you can look for and praise in your child:

Gentleness, loyalty, truthfulness, gratefulness, dependability, creativity, compassion, attentiveness, diligence, humility, generosity, forgiveness, enthusiasm, endurance, boldness, contentment, flexibility, initiative, and faith.

In order to remind myself to praise my children's character, I purchased a poster from Character First! (*character-first.com*). The poster has forty-nine character traits listed with their definitions. My husband and I hung it in a place where we could not possibly ignore it—our bathroom door—to remind ourselves of the different traits we wanted to acknowledge, praise, and nurture in our children.

HANDRAIL NUMBER TWO: MODEL GRACE

A child's need for acceptance and approval is deep. It is rooted in the fact that we are born in sin. Inside every child, at some point in his development, an inner knowing wakes up to the fact that he or she needs acceptance and approval from God. The need is as real and deep as if it were imprinted on the child's DNA. He may not consciously think of it that way, but the need truly exists, and it is bigger than any parent can possibly meet.

This is a time when children need to experience the grace that is personally extended to them through the Gospel. If they can get their minds around the idea that God loves them, that there is nothing they can do to make God love them more and nothing they can do to make God love them less, then they can begin to understand His grace. Grace is the only commodity that can truly meet their deepest need for approval and acceptance.

Raise Eagles, Not Chickens!

Kids learn by what is modeled. How parents *live* in front of them is much more important than what parents *tell* them to do or believe.

Someday I want to write a book called *You Don't Raise Children Like You Raise Chickens*. I have raised chickens and reared children, so I know what I am talking about! Chickens are fairly easy to raise, especially if you have water and feed reservoirs for them. You can fill the feed and water reservoirs once a week if you have the right situation.

When I was on staff at a large church in charge of the children's ministry department, I knew when some parents dropped their children off for Sunday school, that was all the Christian education they were going to get for the week! The parents were just expecting us to "fill 'em up!"

No, you really don't raise children like you raise chickens. Children are more like eagles. The cliff-dwelling eagle builds a huge nest that can weigh a thousand pounds. It is built with a large, heavy, bony structure and lined all soft and comfy. When the eaglets hatch, the mother eagle will perch on the edge of the cliff and flex her wings up and down, up and down. She does this every day. She is modeling, for her little eaglets' eyes, the motions of flight. If she did not do this, her little eaglets would never learn to fly. They would have to walk around the earth like chickens!

When I first heard this I didn't believe it; I tried to verify it through a second source. A friend of mine has a brother who works with wildlife for the Alaska state government. I asked her if she would check to see if what I'd heard was true or not. He positively affirmed it to be true, not only in nature but also in captivity. He knows some wildlife experts who, when working with orphaned baby eaglets, would stand in front of the eaglets and move *their* arms with the motions an adult eagle makes in flight. He admitted their substitute modeling was not nearly as effective as the mother's, but it was the only chance the eaglets had to learn to fly.

In order for our children to be able to grasp huge concepts like God's grace, we must *model* the concept to them much more than we talk to them about it. Best of all, they need to *experience* grace by how they are treated in the family.

Some practical ways to model grace are:

Apologize (Gladly) When You're Wrong

This communicates that it is okay to be wrong. Sometimes we parents act like apologizing causes internal bleeding, and this tells our kids it's unthinkable or abominable to be wrong. Practice apologizing in the mirror. Does it hurt? (If it does, you need to see a doctor!)

Apologizing is simple. There are only three basic ingredients to a good apology:

1. I'm sorry.
2. I was wrong.
3. Here is how I will work to not let it happen again.

Apologizing gladly is such a great back-door way to teach grace. You should rejoice the next time you are wrong, because you've just been handed a golden opportunity to model grace!

My husband graciously taught me how to apologize by modeling it. I was stubborn in our early married years. Once I realized I had been wrong, I'd quickly throw out a distraction—do something funny or crazy. ("Hey, look at the flock of turtles!") On the other hand, when my husband realized he was wrong, he'd quickly apologize and then move on.

That was a mystery to me because I assumed that apologies *cost* something. But my husband could apologize and then go on like he hadn't lost anything. One day my husband asked me why I resisted apologizing so much. I would never have verbalized it at the time, but I really felt like I *couldn't* spit out an apology—that if I tried I would choke right there in the living room, turn purple, and die! My husband gently took me through a quick course on apologizing using logic.

What do you lose when you apologize? Does it cost any money? Does is hurt? If it does, where does it hurt? What good things happen when you apologize?

A little light bulb went on inside my head. *It's so easy! "I'm sorry. I was wr-wr-wrong! I won't do it again . . . or at least I will sure try not to." How hard was that?*

Once a mother asked me what she should do if she apologized to her daughter but her daughter just said, "So what? Those are only words."

I told her to say, "You're right." It is always good if you can find something to agree with, especially when you are working with teenagers. But I encouraged the mother to continue the conversation by asking, "How can I make the apology more real?" There is something very powerful about modeling a true, humble apology to your children when you have erred. You do not diminish in their eyes; curiously, most of the time you will find increased respect as a result.

If you've been acting like apologizing causes internal bleeding, check yourself: Do you truly understand grace? Have you really accepted it in your life? If not, seek a greater understanding—quick. When we are reluctant to apologize, we generally are lacking in the grace department.

Pair Correction With Hope

This is another great way to model grace. If you can take the times that your child feels grace the *least* and find a way to permeate that situation with grace, you'll hit a home run! In ordinary circumstances kids feel the least amount of grace when they are being punished. Hey, don't punish your kids ever again! I really mean that. *Discipline* them instead. The difference is grace. Punishment is the desire to make them feel the price of their misbehavior. Discipline is the desire for them to learn positive things from all circumstances, even the negative ones. So every correction needs to be paired with hope.

For instance, when your child is disrespectful to you, you need to respond with an appropriate negative consequence. But the correction can be framed in such a way as to inspire rather than shame. Here's an example:

> "You know the way you talked to me was wrong, but the reason it is wrong is not that I am such a special person. It's because eventually the way you talk to me and act toward me, as your mother/father, is the way you will talk or act toward God! That's why God tells children to respect their parents. And I want so very much for you to

talk to God and act toward God the way He wants you to."

Another powerful way to pair correction with hope is to bring the child's future into the correction process.

I had a mother come up to me on the sixth night of one of my conferences. She said that she tried pairing hope with correction with her fourteen-year-old daughter and it had worked. Instead of the usual lecture she gave her daughter at the sight of her messy bedroom, she sat down with her on top of all the junk on the bed and said, "Do you know why I care about the condition of your room? It's not because I want my house clean. It's because I know you won't always live with us." (At this the daughter perked her head up—her mother *knew* that she was going to grow up!) The mother continued, "I want you to be able to function as a healthy adult, to be responsible for your own home or apartment and enjoy it, to go to college and be a good roommate, to marry and be a considerate wife."

With a great smile on her face, the mother reported how much fun it was to *inspire* her daughter rather than shame her into cleaning her room. And I reminded that mother that the real victory was not won by the outward behavior of cleaning her room but by the fact that her daughter had experienced back-door grace!

Rejoice in Your Child's God-Given Bent

Another way to model grace is not to just accept the fact that your child is different from you—but to admire the differences! There is something wonderful about our children being like us: looking like us, liking the same food, having the same interests. We tend to capitalize on the similarities and discount the differences. Begin to look for the differences in your child and admire them. Your child—his or her personality—is a creation of God! Admire it as you would an extraordinary flower or star constellation.

I had two boys and then my baby girl came. I didn't expect the boys to be like me, but I sure expected the girl to be. As her personality blossomed I kept hemming her in, focusing on the things that were the same in us, quizzing and quizzing her about the things that were different. *Are you sure you don't like Mexican food? Are you sure you don't like that shirt? It's so cute on you!*

Finally my daughter very graciously explained to me that she was different from me. She laid out all the differences. Wow—there were a lot of them. But I noticed that none of the differences were right or wrong issues. So I began to appreciate her knack for remembering numbers (numbers just leak right out of my head). I remember phone numbers by the melody of the tone most of the time; it's easier, but it's not very effective. I can get it all messed up if the radio is on.

My daughter could remember someone's phone number so easily that she became a walking telephone book for our whole family. She eagerly got her hands on a Palm Pilot when none of our other children had one or knew how to operate one. She programmed her life into it and then she *really* became a family resource. She could pull up just about any random information we might happen to need. I learned to admire her differences and praise the character I saw shining through those traits. Diligence, organization, and attentiveness to detail were just some of the character traits I would otherwise have overlooked had I not been looking to admire the ways she was different from me.

The Bible admonishes us to train up our children in their

own God-given bent (Proverbs 22:6). He made them different from us because if He had made them the same, one of us would be redundant and therefore unnecessary.

Rejoicing in your child's uniqueness models grace because it communicates that it's okay to be unique. And it needs to be okay with us for them to be unique because they already are!

Talk About Others With Grace

Talking about other people's lives is not always gossip; it can actually be helpful as your child learns about the world.

A good rule of thumb we have used is the idea that gossip is being interested and concerned about the *information* in a situation. Non-gossip talking is when there are known facts about a person you know and care about that are appropriate and helpful to talk about. The interest and care is focused on the *person,* not the *information.*

For example, if your good friends file for divorce, some of the topics that would be helpful to discuss with your children (depending on their age and understanding) are:

You don't need to worry about Mommy and Daddy getting a divorce because . . .

Here are some ways that we can show care and sensitivity to this family right now. . . .

Why do you think God doesn't like divorce? (Torn families, broken hearts, disordered society)

The list could go on, but the crucial element to modeling grace in this situation is that you *talk with people about grace.* Somehow you need to find a way to consistently communicate that your highest hope for them is always for reconciliation and restoration. There is a whole chapter in First Corinthians outlining how we are to treat others even when evil is present. "Love is very patient and kind, never jealous or envious, never boastful or proud, never haughty or selfish or rude. Love does not demand its own way. It is not irritable or touchy. It does not hold grudges and will hardly even notice when others do it wrong. It is never glad about injustice, but rejoices whenever truth wins out. *If you love someone you will be loyal to him no matter what the cost.* You will always believe in him, always expect the best of him, and always stand your ground in defending him" (1 Corinthians 13:4–7 TLB, emphasis added).

I've seen this to be possible in even the worst-case scenario. In the middle of the greatest crisis in her family, a grown woman, dealing with the fact that her brother had just been found guilty of molesting a child, demonstrated to me a beautiful example of modeling grace. At the point in the process that she spoke to me, I'm sure she felt like bypassing the legal process and just sending her brother out to be hanged! But in spite of her initial human reaction, she reminded me about an old radio program she used to listen to called *Unshackled*.

Unshackled was produced and aired years ago by the Union Gospel Mission. The Mission took in people whose lives had been broken through all kinds of wicked behavior and abuse. They took them in, fed them, and shared the Gospel with them. Their radio program was the dramatic telling of the remarkable stories of reconciliation and restoration.

My friend continued, "Yes, what my brother did was wrong. But there are more chapters in his book. *If he chooses,* his life could be like one of those *Unshackled* stories."

I find that wherever grace is invited, God peeks in. The clouds part and the sun peeks through, creating that famous silver lining. The people you talk about around your dinner table may never take advantage of the grace God has to offer. But the value in seasoning all of your conversations about others with grace is that you will be modeling grace like that mother eagle models flying to her young!

None of us wants our unmarried daughter to come to us and tell us she is pregnant.

None of us wants our son to come to us and tell us he is addicted to drugs or that he's contemplating suicide.

But if your unwed daughter *is* pregnant or your son *is* addicted to drugs or contemplating suicide, *wouldn't you want them to tell you?*

The best hope you have for keeping communication lines open in a worst-case scenario with your children is that you have laid a *foundation of grace* by consistently talking about others with grace at your kitchen table. How did you talk about the girl in the youth group who got pregnant at fourteen? How did you talk about the boy at school who was addicted to drugs? How did you talk about the neighbor who tried to commit suicide last Christmas?

Kids are smart. You can preach what you think or want to believe, but you will live and model what you *truly believe.* Kids know that. I think they come equipped with little truth detectors!

Continue or Begin to Display Physical Affection

Do you think physical affection is optional? If it is, then why do babies who are denied physical touch die?

Physical affection is essential to communicating acceptance

and grace to your child. Our culture communicates that once children head toward their teenage years, parents should begin to downplay physical affection with them. But nothing could be farther from the truth! Backing off in physical affection is translated by them as *rejection*. If parents begin to sense that their child is backing off physically, they may need to be creative in showing their affection. Grab that boy by the arm and tell him you love him. Sometimes teenage guys don't need you to stop hugging them; they just need you to make those hugs a little more burly. In other words, they may not want wimpy hugs anymore.

Fathers tend to back off from hugging their daughters when their daughters begin to physically develop. I tell them, "Get over it!" Usually all I have to do is remind them that physical affection is a *need,* and their daughter probably has dozens of guys who will take care of her need for physical affection if he doesn't.

Pedophiles look for children who are "thirsty" for physical affection. In some ways children are like sheep. Sheep need still (unmoving) water to drink. They can be walking by a river and either it doesn't register in their little sheep brains that the moving stuff is water, or they dislike drinking from it so much they just refuse it. Instead, if they are thirsty enough when they see a hoofprint that happens to be filled with sheep urine, hey . . . to them it is "still" water and they will drink it. If children don't get what they need, they will be like those thirsty sheep—they will be vulnerable to all kinds of unthinkable evil.

If your children are still young, you may be amazed by their continued openness to physical affection for years to come if you make a decision now that you will not back away from it when they become teenagers. If you never back away, they probably won't either, providing you continue to nurture a good relationship with them.

A few years ago I read a surprising research fact regarding physical affection. The research revealed that farming families in years past did not need to have the level of physical affection that we need today in order to maintain a healthy family. The research did not explore why this would be true. But as I thought about it, it made sense. Families who live together and work side by side together every day hardly ever part company. So I decided that I would use that research to help me remember when to display physical affection to my family members: when my children go off to school and when they come home, when my husband goes to and comes back from work. That can be a simple way to remind yourself to physically express your love. Basically, anytime you part and anytime you come back together!

Look For an Opportunity to Arrange a Grace Experience

What does that mean?

I invented the "Grace Experience" when my oldest child was seven. I would recommend you do this only once or twice in each child's lifetime. The scenario needs to be this: Pick a time when your child totally and completely deserves to be punished. There must be no question in the child's mind that he *deserves* punishment. It's best if it is a situation in which your righteous anger is stirred and you know he really needs to be punished.

With all these constellations lined up, you are ready for a Grace Experience.

Take the child into a quiet room in your house—the formal living room or an office, someplace you will not be disturbed. Talk about what the child did that was wrong and then carefully lay out the punishment you have determined to be appropriate. Make sure the child understands what he has done and what the punishment is to be.

Then you can say, "About that punishment . . . Well, that's what would happen *normally,* but today is different. Today I want to teach you about grace. Grace is an amazing gift that I can't possibly put into words. The best way for you to really begin to learn about grace is to *experience* it. So in a minute I am going to walk out of this room and you can sit here for as long as you want, or just until I am gone. But when you get up, I want you to walk through the doorway of this room and feel what it is like not to have any consequences for what you've done. And I want you to know that I will never bring up this situation in conversation . . . ever! It will be as if it *never happened.* That's what God's grace is like."

Be careful not to preach. Do this with as few words as possible. I believe the Holy Spirit will do the rest. It is a very powerful experience. And you will probably experience a little grace too as you walk out of the room.

Why have I spent so much time dealing with ways to help your child experience grace? Because I believe children learn by experience and modeling far better than they learn by lecture. In fact, did you know that children who are three to eight years old have *double* the brain connections that we do as adults? Because of this fact, children who experience brain injury at this age fare much better than adults with a similar injury. They are able to not only survive a hemispherectomy (the removal of half of the brain), but they can actually function at a relatively normal capacity following this surgery.

But as children enter pre-adolescence and adolescence, they begin a "pruning" process. Brain connections can be pruned up to one thousand per second! What's important for us as parents to know is that *the connections that are NOT pruned are the ones that have been nourished by personal experience.* So we must ensure that really important concepts are personally experienced by our children.

We've been talking here about grace. Making sure you attend a church that teaches grace is not enough. Ideally, in order for a child to personally experience grace, it needs to take place in the culture of the home. Remember, it is those things that are personally experienced that are not pruned away in the brain's pruning phase.

Stage Three is an exceptionally interesting stage regarding grace because people *need* grace before they can *understand* it. Parents who can create an atmosphere of grace at home are more likely to build the foundation necessary for their children to finally begin to understand God's grace.

Summary: Chapter Five

At Stage Three the motive behind decisions is the desire for acceptance.

Important concepts learned at Stage Three:

- A person's value does not change, regardless of behavior or circumstance.

- Everyone needs grace.

Handrails for getting off the Stage Three island:

1. Praise character (Connect good behavior to their fixed character—who they are)

2. Model Grace
   Ways to model grace:

   - Apologize gladly when you're wrong

   - Pair correction with hope

   - Rejoice in your child's God-given bent

   - Talk about others with grace

   - Be physically affectionate

   - Arrange for a "Grace Experience"

CHAPTER 6

Stage Four—The Island of Majority Rules

"Is it normal?"

"But that's not fair!"

Anyone who has parented a child has heard those words. Many times when I would hear my children say those words I'd beam with pride. My child . . . yes! *My* child had figured out that huge universal concept all by himself! What more could a parent hope for?

My children, however, were never amused by this response. They were entering a stage at which a strong sense of justice was preeminent and injustice was a serious matter.

While the use of this phrase ("That's not fair!") is not a summary of Stage Four, it does express the equality expected at Stage Four thinking.

Stage Four is called Majority Rules because here children or adults have matured to the point where they feel *equal* with the rest of the human race. It is more mature than Stage Three because in Stage Three the group existed (at least to the individual) to meet his or her needs. Stage Four makes the big leap to the idea that the individual actually exists to meet the needs of the group.

A perfect example of Stage Four societal order is democracy. Democracy is a system of social equality. All persons are to be treated equally and have an equal vote in determining society's direction. It's a simple system, but it can be immensely popular with anyone who has tasted the bitterness of tyranny or dictatorships, which is government at Stage One!

Important Differences in This Stage

It is wonderful to watch children obey authority, isn't it? It is even more wonderful to watch the *motivations behind that obedience* change from Stage One (fear of punishment) to Stage Two (anticipation of reward) to Stage Three (conforming to be accepted) and then on to Stage Four (respect for law).

The beauty of individuals operating at Stage Four is that they are beginning to develop an understanding of the mutuality that needs to exist between people in a civilized world. In terms of how that would look in your home, the rules of the home are respected *for their own sake* and not because you are standing behind those rules with punishment, reward, or acceptance as the consequence of their conformity or nonconformity to the rules.

People who have reached Stage Four are much healthier in their view of themselves and others than those who are operating at Stage Three, because people who are motivated by issues in Stage Three are at the mercy of those from whom they are seeking acceptance.

THE DOWNSIDE OF STAGE FOUR

Like all the other stages, this one has a downside. The person who is operating at Stage Four is asking, "Is it normal?" What's wrong with that question? Well, the trouble is that what is considered "normal" *changes*. A hundred years ago it was normal to wait to have sex until married. Now it is normal to have sex and even cohabitate before marriage. And to act outside the norm is considered deviant, which invites ridicule and shunning by other people in our society. One hundred years ago it was deviant to have sex before marriage, and those who did were criticized and shunned. Now it is *deviant* (i.e., deviates from society) to wait until after marriage to have sex. When I speak at school assemblies or youth groups and I get to this part of my talk, the students respond with nods. They know exactly what I am talking about!

To think of deliberately killing a baby in the womb fifty years ago was considered outrageous by most. Today it is the norm to think that abortion is a choice that should be given to women.

Not that all in the past was perfect. Many people accepted slavery as being a normal part of their culture 150 years ago. Was it good? No, but it was normal to large groups of people!

People operating in Stage Four have done a lot of unspeakable things. Stage Four can feel so civilized that logical people can be pulled into agreeing with illogical reasoning or participating in acts that, at another place and time, they would deplore. For example, Hitler's regime operated at Stage Four. Every action Hitler took was first made legal according to German law. Really nice people operating at Stage Four made it possible for Hitler and his regime to commit unspeakable atrocities.

How did he get nice people to follow him?

He brought order to an economy that was shattered by World War I. He played statesman so well that reasonable people were drawn into his scheme—people who were operating in the "norm" mode, that is. The world still marvels that such reasonable people voted and participated in a system that was so evil at its heart. That is just one example from history that shows *anything* can be made normal.

When the top leaders in Hitler's regime were brought to trial for the war crimes they had committed, many of them defended themselves by stating that all of the things they had done were legal at the time. If the international committee in charge of the trial had been operating at Stage Four, all of those charged would have been deemed innocent! But the committee predetermined they could not operate at Stage Four when they considered the evidence. They had to bump up their moral consideration to Stage Five in order to come up with the right rulings. So, like Stages One through Three, Stage Four also is only an island to travel through, not an island to build your life on.

If people stop developing and get stuck on the Stage Four island, they will be vulnerable to the majority vote. The idea that "if the majority agrees then it must be right" is dangerous. The Bible teaches us that people can be like sheep—following one another blindly, which is somewhat the essence of Stage Four. It's wonderful if the lead sheep is going the right direction, but it's disastrous if she isn't.

We see in the Bible how the crowd wanted Jesus to be their king and then a few short days later wanted Him crucified. There is a danger in following the crowd. Might doesn't make right, and numbers don't guarantee a desired direction. The broad road does not end up at the best destination from God's point of view.

Another downside of Stage Four is an individual's lack of understanding regarding laws. A Stage Four person will think that laws come from what everyone has agreed to. But good laws are not drafted from opinion polls. Good laws are based on *principles*. We need to teach our children the difference between laws and principles: Principles are the roots and trunk of the tree, while laws are the branches. Good laws sprout up from the principles. Children need to know early on that good laws have universal reasons behind them.

Of course, it is much more work for a parent to teach principles and their connection to rules. Rules are easier to grasp, teach, and enforce, while principles take lots of explanation and have to be interpreted in different circumstances. But I'm getting ahead of myself; that is a subject for chapter eight.

Ways to Help Your Child Move Beyond Stage Four

Moving beyond Stage Four is very difficult in today's secular culture. If each stage is an island and each island is linked to the next by bridges, we must realize that the bridge between Stage Four and Stage Five has been blown up in recent years! The bomb that blew up the bridge came in the form of two secular ideas:

1. There is no absolute truth.

2. Man is basically good.

So how does a parent help his or her teenager mature beyond Stage Four? Since there is now no bridge teenagers can take, with handrails to help them across, we need another strategy for their continued moral development. They must learn how to *swim!*

SWIM LESSON #1: CHALLENGE THEM

Teenagers need a challenge! Many times as parents we help them too soon and smooth their way, not realizing that they do not need comfort as much as they need *purpose.*

The Marines have an interesting recruiting poster. It reads:

We Could Promise You Sleep Deprivation,
Mental Torment
And Muscles So Sore You'll Puke . . .
But We Don't Want To Sugarcoat Things.

Marines are the most prestigious branch of the U.S. armed forces among American teenagers. Why? Because the Marines know that teenagers are up to a challenge.

Meanwhile, Christian parents can too often focus their concern on whether or not their teen is *having fun* at youth group. Churches many times host fun event after fun event . . . like pizza parties with five-minute devotions . . . and may even apologize for the devotions.

Teens are not only up to a challenge, they *need* a challenge. And what better challenge can there be than the challenge to leave the norm and learn to be a Stage Five thinker?

Some practical ways to challenge teenagers are:

Stop asking "Did You Have Fun?" after every event

Asking this communicates that you value fun as the ultimate goal for them. Parents have shredded many youth pastors because their youth came home complaining that they weren't having enough fun! The poor youth pastor didn't go to Bible school or get a ministry degree to become a fun-event planner. Sometimes the greatest disciplines of the faith are not best described as fun. Enriching—yes, thought-provoking—yes, stirring—yes, but probably not fun.

A better question might be, "What did you learn or do?" And then go from there.

Seek faith-stretching experiences

As your children become teenagers, it is important that their faith become their own. This can be a nail-biting experience for parents because they have to let go a little and let their teen really see that God wants to work *directly with them.*

Two years ago my sixteen-year-old daughter decided she wanted to go on a mission trip during her summer vacation. We had already enrolled her in a summer camp. There was no possible way financially we could send her on the mission trip as well. However, we suggested that she pray about the decision. We didn't have a problem with her going; we trusted the people in charge of the trip. My husband and I could have wrestled with the decision ourselves, but we realized that our daughter was getting to the age where she needed to learn how God leads in personal decision making.

She knew that if God led her to make the decision to go, He would also have to provide the money for the trip. She really agonized over the decision. In the middle of the process she asked me, "How do you know it is God wanting you to do something if you yourself want it also? How do you know God is saying go and it's not your own mind?" What great questions. We encouraged her to "lay the trip down"—in other words, give up on the idea and see if God gave it back. She did.

Two weeks after the deadline for signing up I thought she had decided not to go on the trip, but she asked me to call the church and see if she could still sign up. The church was happy to put her name on the list, but now the pressure was really on. Not on her parents, of course! We calmly watched to see what God would do to build the faith of our daughter. It would have to be a miracle. She had committed to teaching Vacation Bible School, then she had ten free days until the summer camp started, after which she would come home and then leave for the mission trip in Mexico. What person would want to hire a teen for just ten days in the summer? And how could she possibly make the amount needed in a mere ten days?

Around the time that school let out for the summer, my daughter performed in a school musical. One of the ladies who attended the musical approached her after the program and asked if she might be interested in a job. She said she really felt God was directing her to hire Robyn. She went on to explain that it was a different kind of job—a very short job but with good pay and good hours for the days she could work. In fact, the job was only *ten days* in the summer and involved running a fireworks stand. I bet you can guess which days those ten days were! Believe it or not, they were the exact ten days our daughter had free. (And I bet you can imagine how much money she made in regard to how much she needed!) Robyn learned so much from this *very* personal experience in how God leads and provides.

My husband and I learned from the experience as well. We learned that no matter how much parents love their children and desire to see their faith grow and become their own, no one wants this to happen more than God! He will make himself real to those who are just learning to trust Him if He is given the opportunity.

Sometimes faith-stretching experiences can be painful. If we're not careful as parents, we can rescue our kids from what we see as a painful situation that God *could have used* to really stretch their faith. Our daughter was in agony over her decision to go on the mission trip. It was so tempting for us to just rescue her. It's important to look more deeply at the painful situations in our children's lives. Sometimes we do need to intervene, but sometimes God is using it for something far greater.

When I was a kid (a really long time ago), my father worked for a university in Davis, California. They held a special day there once a year called Picnic Day, and to me it seemed like everyone in the world attended. All the scientists and professors were there with various experiments and displays to look at. There was a cow that had a glass window in its side, which allowed us to peer directly into its stomach. There was a whole kennel of dogs that were de-barked. It really gave me an odd feeling to walk past them. They apparently did not know they could not bark; the dogs continued to bark, but there was no sound coming out.

Anyway, there was one area where people could watch chicks hatch. There were chicks hatching all day long. At the end of one particular Picnic Day, my father caught the scientists tossing the unhatched eggs down the garbage disposal. (Hey, guys, this was the early 1970s.) From then on my dad brought the unhatched eggs home for us to hatch and raise.

This was not done to spare their little lives as much as to avoid the waste. We ate them months later.

We were usually dog tired from what was probably the biggest event of the year for us, but we'd stay up late and watch those eggs because we knew in a short twenty-four hours they would all be hatched.

One year my sister and I were watching one particular little chick. He was so small and weak; his little eyelids were closed and transparent over his bulging eyes. He was working so hard to crack open his shell and get out. We took pity on him, thinking that no little chick should have to go through so much. So we helped him.

You know what happened?

He died.

Little chickens have big, heavy heads. They have to have strong necks to lift their heads and eat and drink. They don't automatically come with strong necks; their necks *become strong* as they agonizingly sweat their way out of the little oval cage God put them in.

We need to see the whole picture when we look at the pain in our kids' lives too. Do we value their comfort more than we value their character? Do we want them to be soothed more than we want them to be strong? There is no reason to value pain itself, but there is a great reason to value its by-products: patience, character, and hope. Part of seeking faith-stretching experiences for your children is seeing pain in perspective and not short-circuiting important experiences for them just because the situations aren't pleasant at the moment.

Invest in their spiritual training

Another way to challenge those stuck at Stage Four to swim for the Mainland (Stages Five and Six) is to invest in their spiritual training. One of the things I encourage parents to do is send their child to a top-notch biblical worldview summer camp. I have one that I particularly recommend called Worldview Academy Leadership Camp (*www.worldview. org*). I take brochures for the camp everywhere I go to speak so that parents can check it out. It's not just for kids interested in leadership. It's for kids who need to get a better idea how to have a personal relationship with Christ through daily devotions, etc. It also gives kids practical, easy-to-remember tools to help them survive with their faith fresh and intact, no matter where they go for college. All this can be accomplished because the goal of the leaders is not to tell the kids *what* to think but to teach them *how* to think—a skill that can serve them anywhere they go.

When parents see the cost of the camp, many times they immediately discount it as a viable option for their family. They are used to sending their kids to church camp, which is often underwritten by the church family and the true cost is not reflected in the price. However, if the leadership camp were a sports camp or a music camp, they would not have the same sticker shock. What does the child think when his or her parents are willing to spend money on a secular camp but not a Christian camp? I don't know how much money you have to spend on extracurricular events for your children, but I would encourage you to see opportunities for biblical worldview training as high on your priority list.

On the other hand, investing in your child's spiritual training doesn't have to cost money; the cost may be in time and creativity. When interesting Christian leaders come to town, take your teenager to hear them speak. We did that many times, and often our kids were the only people under eighteen at the conferences. We would happily pull them out of school, and they were more than happy to be pulled out to do something different. We always encouraged our kids to go up front afterward and talk with the speakers. Many times, because they were kids, the leaders would give them extra time and attention.

One of the speakers our kids got to know came to speak at their school for an assembly. The students were all excited about it and our kids were able to say, "Yeah, we know him. We had lunch with him last year." Twice our kids were pulled out of school for Peter Lowe's conferences. They were the only kids in an entire stadium of people, but they heard an incredible lineup of speakers all day long. Our kids went to a John Maxwell leadership conference when they were in grades five, six, and eight. And in grades seven, eight, and ten they went to a George Barna conference. When kids are skipping school to go to a conference with their parents it's amazing how interested they become in the speaker's talks!

Getting your teenager to an understanding of Stage Five (principles) thinking is quite contrary to the direction of the culture. If your children are in any kind of contact with the outside world (television, school, movies, music), it takes significant effort to counter the tide of cultural messages. Maturity in decision making is too vital to be left to chance. Don't be afraid to bring in outside help and don't be reluctant to invest time and money if there is a chance of impacting your child's spiritual development.

Allow yourself to be stretched and refined

Ouch! Parenting teenagers can be painful. They are innate "hypocrisy detectors." As parents of younger children, you may have been able to get away with duplicity. There were probably many times when you did not want your child to hear or see things that were not appropriate for their age. But it was okay, maybe even necessary, for you to hear or see those same things. The nightly news, for one example, is usually not good for small children to watch. So parents of young children get into the mindset of "It's okay for me but not for you."

However, I think parents of teens need to make a shift in this department. If you don't want your teen watching or hearing something, you probably shouldn't be viewing it or listening to it either! This can be very refining when put into practice. The value of shifting gears is that you move from duplicity to integrity in the eyes of your teenager.

After teaching our children *how* to watch and analyze what they watched—movies or TV shows—we found that they were really good at it. In fact, they were better than we were! We learned to humble ourselves and turn off the program by the same rules we were encouraging them to use as they watched media and entertainment.

SWIM LESSON #2: ENGAGE THE CULTURE

For younger children it is important that they learn all the great stories in the Bible. But when kids get to be teenagers, the typical curriculum for their Christian education needs to be stretched. With the Bible for a foundation, teens need to be encouraged to *apply biblical principles* as they engage the current culture. There are Christian news magazines that are helpful, but it is important that any resources you use focus more on teaching teens *how* to think than telling them *what* to think! Teens need to experience the wrestling process of taking biblical principles and wrapping them around current issues. It can sometimes be mind stretching. The reason that this exercise is so important is because when your teen is middle-aged and at his highest point of influence in society, the issues will probably be completely different than they are now. Knowing *how* to translate principles into specific issues will be critical.

When encouraging your teens to engage the culture, it is important that you educate them on the powerful influences that are out there. Television is a huge influence. This is because of how the brain reacts when watching it. When a person watches TV his brain activity virtually shuts down on the left side as all the activity is switched to the right side. This happens so quickly that the body actually releases endorphins as a result of the rapid brain shift. This would account for television's addictive element for some people.

The real trouble is that the left side is the side of the brain in charge of critical thinking skills. The right side is like a small child, open to impressions and suggestions. When the news of this research hit the streets, it was the advertisers that paid the most attention to it. They realized that if the research was true, they no longer had to worry about *content* in advertising. The advertiser could merely work to make an impression on the right brain and their job would be done. Aha! That might explain some of the weird commercials, eh? Who knew a lizard could sell insurance?

My husband and I wanted to counteract the influence of television and movies in our children's lives without entirely removing them from our lives. So we began to challenge our kids to keep the left side of their brain awake. We questioned them after movies with questions like: "What was the worldview or overall message?" This has become a habit in our home. Everyone knows that after the movie there will be a test! It's actually a fun family game we play, a mental challenge in abstract and interpretive thinking.

Rethink your rating system for media

Many times parents rate movies by a linear list of outward behaviors. Do the characters use foul language? Is there graphic or glorified violence portrayed? Are there inappropriate sexual scenes or sex between unmarried people? These issues are important, but sometimes we strain at a gnat and swallow a camel. Obviously we use the above criteria for choosing movies, but we look deeper at the overall *message* of the film or TV show. For Christians parents, this may be the most important criteria of all in ranking entertainment for our children.

I have a whole section in my parenting conferences where we go through various movies and assess their worldview. It took me a lot of practice before the skill came easily. But it is a powerful exercise, not just in assessing the "bad" movies but also finding the movies with an excellent message. We must never lose sight of the power of that media and how it can impact our families, both positively and negatively.

I hope you have been encouraged to challenge your teenager to muster the mental effort it takes to swim to Stage Five—the Mainland. If you are able to create an understanding, a love, and a commitment to biblical principles in your teen's heart, you have really accomplished something in the current culture!

Summary: Chapter Six

Decisions at Stage Four are motivated by the desire to be normal, to agree with the majority.

The important concept learned at Stage Four:
A healthy respect for the law, not out of fear of punishment but out of an understanding that law and order, which bring civilized society, are good for everyone.

There is no bridge off the Stage Four island, so you must encourage your children to jump off and *swim* to the Mainland of Stages 5 and 6. Some of the best ways we can do this are:

SWIM LESSON #1: CHALLENGE THEM

- Stop asking "Did you have fun?" after every event (this question keeps them at the "norm" as far as expectations are concerned).

- Seek faith-stretching experiences.

- Invest in their spiritual training.

- Allow *yourself* to be stretched and refined (model spiritual growth).

SWIM LESSON #2: ENGAGE THE CULTURE

- Ask: What is the message of this media program, and is it true?

CHAPTER 7

Level Two—It's All About Us!

You'll remember that back in chapter four we discussed the Stage One and Stage Two islands, whose main motivation in making decisions was, "It's All About Me." Together they made up Level One. Moving beyond that, we then looked at Stage Three and Stage Four, whose motivation changed from *me* to *us*. That's the main difference between Level One and Level Two: *other people*!

When individuals progress to Stage Three and Stage Four (Level Two), they begin to regard others when making decisions. This is a huge step from the total self-centeredness of the first two islands. It's important for older children and teenagers to be able to operate at this level. But we all know that modern culture promotes self-centeredness. Taking others into consideration before making a decision, or having the capacity to sympathize or empathize with others, is a highly desirable goal to reach with our children.

However, we mustn't let the relatively more mature Level

Two fool us into being content to stay there. As desirable as it is for children to begin to regard others in their decisions, the maturity level and motive behind Level Two are still off the mark. Its premise, "It's all about *us,*" has two problems: it's not true, and it stops short of God's desire for us. Maturity in Christ can only happen when we realize that it's *not* all about us—there is a larger-than-life God who eclipses all the plans, accomplishments, and dreams of all people throughout all time and space.

It's like we're in a scripted play that we assume is all about us. As we take our places and say our lines, we assume that *we* are the main characters. Then, over time, questionable events occur or maybe a sudden twist in the script makes us question the director. "Why did this person die?" Or "Why did that person lose his job?" It doesn't make sense as far as the direction we were expecting the script to take. If we really pay attention, it can slowly dawn on us that in this particular play, the play of life, we are not the main characters. The main character is God! He is also the director and producer. And this play has been going on for thousands of years. We play a few roles in various scenes and then our part is done. But the play will continue for . . . well, we don't know how long. Only the director knows.

When we think of it that way our perspective changes. We no longer have to scour our worn little scripts for the "happily ever after" scene. That scene is at the very end of the play, as it is with most fine plays. If we don't expect it to be here and now, we can then get to the business of playing our parts with the real purpose of the play in mind: *to please and glorify God.*

Now, prepare yourself for the biggest leap a soul can take! Let us leap into the frigid water that laps up on the island of Stage Four and swim with all our strength to Stage Five. I hear it is a magnificent place, very much worth the effort of getting there!

Summary: Chapter Seven

Stages Three and Four make up the "It's All About Us" phase.

Progressing beyond Stage Three and Stage Four is imperative for a Christian because all decisions made at the "It's All About Me" or "It's All About Us" stages do not involve God!

- Level One: It's All About Me!

- Level Two: It's All About Us!

Progressing beyond Level Two is highly important for Christians. God is not even a part of the decision-making process until we reach Stage Five. Moving on to Stages Five and Six (Level Three) allows us to truly serve God in our everyday decisions.

CHAPTER 8

Stage Five—
Self-Evident Truths

"Is it right?"

Welcome to the Mainland, the ultimate destination in maturity! Stage Five is a place where decisions are made by principles based on God's revealed truth to us, either through His word—biblical truth—or through the world He created—self-evident truths or natural law. Although God's written word affirms all truth we might find in His creation, even those with no access to God's written laws are held accountable to His laws, as they are so clearly shown through creation (Romans 1:18–20). Stage Five is all about principles that help us make good decisions that will truly please God.

For teenagers, principled thinking is the difference between making wise choices and developing character or being disrespectful of authority, being enslaved to addictive behaviors, being promiscuous, cheating, lying, or even committing suicide. Such is the power of principled thinking.

At all of the lower stages—Stage One through Stage Four—people are in danger of making bad decisions. But when we are operating at Stage Five, all our decisions are *good* decisions because they are based on self-evident truths that are a part of the way God created the world to operate. For parents to be principled thinkers and to bring up their children to be principled thinkers is the ultimate achievement in Christian parenting.

The Difficult Path to Stage Five

Since Stage Five is part of the Mainland—the ultimate destination—a parent does not need to worry about progressing their child *beyond* the goal of being able to think in principles.

I believe the reason people move through a process or stages of maturity is because God created us to build learning upon learning, one major concept serving as a foundation for the next. We feel the need to progress from stage to stage because the lower levels of reasoning become inadequate as life gets more and more complicated. Higher and higher reasoning needs to take place, or God's design for our development is thwarted. In our current postmodern culture, development between Stages Four and Five is so hindered by secular thought that it makes it incredibly difficult for some to even *understand* Stage Five.

When I speak to younger, more postmodern groups, I have to spend a great deal of time talking about the transition between Stage Four and Stage Five. The reason, I believe, is that our postmodern culture has really embraced the two bombs that blew up the bridge between Stage Four and Stage

Five: "There is no absolute truth" and "Man is basically good and doesn't need God." In fact, that is a pretty good definition of postmodernists: *those who have been disillusioned from believing in real truth or ideals.*

A Stage Five teenager realizes there *is* real truth; there *is* a right and a wrong in life that transcends culture and circumstances. Principles of life, the self-evident truths, do not change. There are many people today who are repelled by the idea of absolute truth, but no matter how much they protest, it does not change the reality of the fact in any way.

To illustrate this, imagine if I were to take a loaded gun in one hand, a bullet in the other, and shoot a bullet straight out of the gun at the exact same time as I dropped the bullet from the other hand. If both were the same height from the ground, which bullet would hit the earth first—the one dropped or the one shot out of the gun?

The truth is, *they would both hit the earth at the same time!*

Why? Because velocity does not change gravity. Objects fall at 9.8 meters per second per second. Period. Just because the bullet shot out of the gun is speeding in a horizontal direction does not mean gravity has been overruled. And so it is with self-evident truths. They exist like gravity exists. It doesn't matter how you feel about them, how everyone votes concerning them, or how distracting the velocity of the culture is to them. Truth is truth.

What is so tragic about postmodernism—embracing the idea that there is no absolute truth—is it keeps young people from developing morally. Remember, one of the suppositions in the beginning was that individuals cannot understand more than one stage above where they are primarily operating. The majority of students today are graduating from high school at Stage Three—Crude Conformity. So the ceiling above Stage

Four keeps them *all the more* from really understanding the idea of principles that can so perfectly guide their decision making.

The highest a teenager can think while primarily at Stage Three is Stage Four. Teenagers operating at Stage Four will be motivated by man-made laws: the good of society with the majority of people going the same direction. But a teenager operating at Stage Five knows that sometimes the majority can be wrong. A Stage Five thinker is interested in what is right according to the original design of the Creator.

At the lower levels of "It's All About Me" or "It's All About Us," the only consideration for discerning truth is ourselves or those around us. Proverbs says, "There is a way that seems right to a man, but in the end it leads to death" (Proverbs 14:12). Those who think at Stage Five know that truth is greater than their own small perspective. It is God's revealed truth that shows us how to live and keeps us from making wrong decisions.

"How can a young man keep his way pure? By living according to your word" (Psalm 119:9). "Your word is a lamp to my feet and a light for my path" (Psalm 119:105). "For the word of God is living and active. Sharper than any double-edged sword, it penetrates even to dividing soul and spirit, joints and marrow; it judges the thoughts and attitudes of the heart" (Hebrews 4:12).

The Unchanging Nature of Principles

While over time our ideas and issues may change, principles *do not change*. The beauty of tried-and-true principles is that they translate down into any culture, circumstance, or issue. The "value of human life" principle touches different issues now than it did centuries ago. Centuries ago several cultures were coming to grips with slavery, and the principle of the "value of human life" was driving that issue. But now that same principle is at the heart of the abortion debate. Issues change, what's "normal" changes, but good principles do not change. That's what makes Stage Five such a great place out of which to make decisions! If you translate the principle well, you are not going to make bad decisions.

Two dynamics of modern culture accentuate the need for our teenagers to become principled thinkers. For one thing, never before has culture changed so *rapidly*. In a fast-changing culture like ours, laws and rules change more quickly as well. How frightening that our fast-changing culture has fewer and fewer principled thinkers at the helm! When the rules or laws need to change, what will be the criteria for change?

The other dynamic that accentuates the need for our teenagers to become principled thinkers is that modern culture has so many toxic elements in it—ways for young people to destroy themselves as they walk on well-traveled paths paved by the culture. STDs, AIDS, self-mutilation, addictions of all kinds, eating disorders, and suicide are just some of the ways kids can do great harm to themselves and others simply by following the sanctioned message from the culture. A teen whose mature heart guides him or her into principled thinking will be able to receive the wisdom and understanding that God so desperately wants to give to all of us.

And so we come to the core of this book. How do we as parents raise up our children—with learning upon learning—to the point that they become principled-thinking teenagers?

Obviously it takes time and maturity to operate at Stage Five consistently. Children are able to exhibit good *outward behavior* at all of the previous stages. Operating at lower stages does not mean that their decisions will all be bad. That's why the Secret Path to Heart Maturity is not focused on outward behavior alone. In order for your teenagers to reach the highest level of heart maturity, they must swim to the Mainland, where their reasoning skills can serve them well *in any circumstance* and lead to consistently good moral decisions.

LET YOUR CHILDREN WATCH YOU MAKE DECISIONS

The best way to draw teenagers more and more to heart maturity is to MODEL Stage Five thinking for them. There is great value in letting your children watch you make decisions. As our children became teenagers, my husband and I involved them in our decisions when it was appropriate. They listened to and participated in our discussions and watched us wrestle with the question, *What is the right thing to do here?*

When you as parents wrestle with decisions, make sure your motivations are not operating at the lower levels. If your children hear you say things like "What will the neighbors think?" or "No one will see—there's no way we'd get in trouble," or "There's nothing wrong with doing that; every other person at work has done the same thing," you can imagine how this will impact them. Talk about getting the wrong message!

As you model decision making, it is vital that you operate at Stages Five and Six. In fact, we found that after our kids knew about the six stages, they were dreadfully good at catching us operating or trying to parent them out of the lower stages. They learned to respectfully make us aware when we were doing it. Ahhh, alas, raising teenagers is so . . . refining!

As parents, we need to remember that we are communicating even when we might not want to be. Our actions communicate our thoughts. It is imperative that we put the effort into parenting at the principle level in our everyday lives.

I often come across parents who parent out of guilt. For some reason, they feel guilty about a circumstance or event that has occurred in their child's life, and it negatively affects the way they interact. They are less apt to enforce boundaries or requirements. They may give extravagant gifts and tiptoe around the child, lest he become unhappy or angry. "Guilt parenting" communicates a principle to children, but not a true principle. It communicates the principle: *We are victims of the events or circumstances of our lives!*

I encourage moms and dads to never parent out of guilt but rather out of *conviction*. Guilt is feeling bad about a divorce, being too busy, a bad situation, an illness or birth defect in a child. Conviction is being convinced that *with God, good can come out of* any *circumstance!* "And we know that in all things God works for the good of those who love him, who have been called according to his purpose" (Romans 8:28). All things may not work for our comfort and happiness, but it is promised that if we love Him, they will work for good for His purpose!

Guilt deals with what happened yesterday. Conviction is deciding what will happen tomorrow. Guilt is a feeling. Conviction is a decision based on *principle*. How important it is that we know how to operate at a principle level! One great principle parents communicate when they switch from "guilt parenting" to "conviction parenting" is this: *We are not a product of our environment. We are a product of the decisions we make.*

Do I believe a child needs both a mother and a father? Absolutely! But do I believe a child who has been the victim of divorce or abandonment is irreparably damaged? Absolutely not! The child will be *different,* but he or she does not have to live a *damaged* life. Parents are so relieved when they realize this truth; it's not the circumstances we have, but what we *do* with the circumstances that makes us who we are. There are plenty of stories about people who have lived through a wide range of horrific experiences or circumstances but have risen up to live extraordinary lives. There are also plenty of people who have been given much and had optimum environments, but they have chosen to live destructive lives. The difference is in which principle they *believe* about the way God designed the world.

That is what it takes to parent with principles. Carefully determine what you *believe* and make sure it is reflected in how you *act.*

ENGAGE THE CULTURE AS YOU SIT, WALK, AND STAND

Deuteronomy 6:7 encourages us to teach our children as we live with them! Use what they see every day as illustrations of God's truth. As you watch current events with your children, you can draw out the principles being honored or neglected. Watch and make judgments about not just whether the act was right or wrong but *why* the act was right or wrong, and then discuss intent and consequences. An extreme example would be that of a woman killing her husband because he was abusing her. First, the offense has to be dealt with. *Was it right or wrong, and* why *was it right or wrong?*

Kids get distracted with the *reason* the woman killed her husband. The more extreme the example, the more distracting the different factors can be. Although intent can play a part in determining the *severity of the punishment,* it does not play a part in determining right or wrong. Right or wrong exists outside of us. Our own little inner motives do not change what is right or wrong.

The answer to the question of right or wrong is that the woman was wrong to kill her husband. The answer to *why* it is wrong is that the civil law (reflecting God's unchanging principle, "Thou shalt not kill") is structured to deal with the woman's problem. She could have used the law to straighten out her problem. Instead, she took the law into her own hands.

Engaging the world with your family will give you excellent opportunities to communicate important principles for decision making.

Practical Modeling of Principles at Home

Besides just looking at the evening news for conversations about principles, parents need to seek opportunities in everyday home life. Great opportunities lie under every crisis or transition.

When our oldest child graduated from high school he was so excited. He was free! Of course, he was still living at home and we were still paying for most of what he needed to survive. We realized he was in need of some *practical understanding* of principles. We could have simply laid down the law and told him that as long as he was at our house, he needed to comply with certain rules—that is, his freedom still had boundaries. Instead of doing that, we took the opportunity to teach him a principle. We sat down at the table and drew it out on paper.

Responsibility ——————————————— Obedience

"See these two words? They are connected. As long as we take responsibility for the house you live in, the car insurance for the car you drive, etc., there is a certain level of obedience due back to us. Of course, the more independent you become, the more your obedience to us turns into honor, which is a completely different word than obedience."

This principle becomes crystal clear if you are in a public place and someone asks you to remove your coat and give it to them . . . and then your personal computer, and your purse or your wallet, then they ask for your shoes . . . And you compliantly give them all they ask for! Why? Because you are at the airport! And the security personnel you are being obedient to are *responsible* for the safety of your flight.

"So," we explained to our son, "as long as we are responsible for different aspects of your care and survival, there is a connecting tie of obedience that goes with that. It's not personal, it's just principle, like physics or math!"

It was so much better than the old "as long as you're under my roof" routine. Now we're no longer responsible for any of his survival needs, but because we used that situation to *teach* him, he was able to take with him a valuable principle that he can use in his own home or work life.

I have been criticized for using the word *obedience* in this illustration; one person felt that teenagers would not respond to the word *obedience*. I agree that it has a negative punch to it in our culture. However, that challenge has made me want to communicate even more to parents the importance of this principle.

Contrary to popular opinion, *obedience* is a great word. Obedience is what God wants in my life. It is not a word reserved for children. In fact, my husband and I tell our children that we are expected to be *more obedient* than they are because if they aren't obedient, their worst consequence would be to get a time-out or be expelled from school. But if we are not obedient we will lose our job or our driver's license or go to prison. Obedience is a great word that the current culture has rejected, much like they have rejected the word *truth*. Our job as parents is not to find a way to reword principles in today's format but to educate our children on the beauty and value of biblical concepts that their culture may not value.

DON'T FORGET THE DEEP ISSUES OF THE HEART

It's important to share life principles that may not directly affect outward behavior but deal with deep issues of the heart. How healthy would America be if parents began to teach their children the principles of forgiveness? How tremendous for a teenager to learn early in life that forgiveness is a *decision*, not a feeling. It is a decision that is made with great precision and careful thought (study the life of Joseph) and will greatly benefit you as you walk with God (study the life of Corrie ten Boom).

The challenge in teaching principles to your teen is for you to know the principles yourself! The Bible obviously is your greatest resource. The book of Proverbs is a book of principles that was written for the purpose of training young people. I have also found a great principle-based, character education program that I use and recommend called Character First! (*characterfirst.com*).

Character education is a hot topic these days, but it has been around for a long time. When done well, it teaches biblical principles that guide all the decisions of life.

Teaching biblical principles as you go through life (as you sit, walk, and lie down) can give your child and eventually your teenager the materials to construct the foundation on which the rest of his or her life can be built.

The Moment of Opportunity

So what does the opportunity to share a life principle with your teenager look like? Any time you are faced with a decision regarding your teen, or your teen is wrestling with an issue or problem, is a prime opportunity. If we truly want to raise principled-thinking teenagers, we need to take a flying leap at this point—a leap from rules to principles. Instead of telling teenagers what they should do in a particular situation (the rule), we need to shift gears and share the overarching principles of God's world with them, then sit back as *they* wrestle with the principles to translate them down into their own lives.

I encourage parents to take their teenagers to a "third place" if possible to have this discussion. Starbucks, for instance, calls itself a third place, since it is not home or work or school. It is a place where there are no chores, no bills to pay, and no agendas to accomplish. It is a *great* place for parents to have pivotal conversations with their teenagers. Being in a third place can help both the parent and the teen by removing unconnected agendas and distractions.

My husband and I chose a nearby coffee shop. We found our teenagers were always quick to set aside other activities to meet with us at a coffee shop. Being in a third place helped us to remember that we were transitioning a child to become an adult; our job as parents was not to solve our children's problems but to make sure they had the principles to solve their own problems. I am a very visual person and found that many times it helped both of us when I would draw the principle on a napkin. Here are some of the principles I've used:

Responsibility _____ Obedience

(Obedience is due to those who take responsibility for your life or an aspect of it.)

We've discussed this principle earlier in the chapter. It's helpful with a child who assumes he or she has outgrown the need to be obedient to anyone. He's reached a certain age (usually eighteen), and he thinks he's no longer responsible to anyone. Many times teenagers think that if the world labels them an adult, they have outgrown all boundaries. How far from the truth this is!

Freedom _____ Self-Control

(Freedom is linked to self-control. The more self-control a person or nation has, the more freedom they can enjoy.)

This can be used when children expect freedom because they see other kids their age gaining greater freedom. They assume that freedom is given indiscriminately according to age. This principle shows them that freedom is not linked to any certain age (look at prisoners as one example). Rather, it is linked to self-control. This is true whether talking about an individual or a nation. For this reason, free nations must cherish and promote self-control in order to continue to be free.

Joy (true happiness) _____ Purpose

(Joy can transcend any circumstance if there is significant purpose.)

Athletes punish their bodies through training because they

have a great purpose. Our teenagers often resist the punishment of self-discipline. They assume they are trading self-discipline for happiness. But true happiness (joy) has nothing to do with pain or pleasure. It has to do with purpose. If the purpose is great enough, joy can transcend any pain or drudgery we may feel. This principle is important when parents are trying to motivate their teen to make decisions for their future. It's helpful to start with the "purpose" for the discipline you are hoping to see them embrace.

Parents who "leap" from parenting with rules to parenting with principles will be equipping their child for life! Giving teens a biblical principle at such an impressionable age will strongly increase the odds that it will stay with them and guide them for the rest of their lives.

An Important Last Point

At this stage in the journey you might conclude that I am saying your child can take a "human development" path to "goodness." This is not possible from what we know to be true, according to those unchanging facts we call theology. So for those of you who are poised and ready to call the theology police, let me explain how I understand the parents' role in raising "good" kids.

The best way I have found to clarify what is really happening as God matures our children's hearts, draws them to himself, and gives them power to make good moral decisions is to reference a chapter in the book of Job. Chapter 28 is a pinnacle passage in Job. It paints a picture of people who live and walk around on the earth, people who know that under the ground are mystifyingly valuable and rare formations like sapphires, onyx, topaz, rubies, and jasper. Since people know about these things and value them, they go to great lengths to obtain them. They go far into the lonely places of the earth, dig deep holes, and dangle from ropes down in the holes, hoping to extract what they have come to regard as highly valuable.

Then Job contrasts this picture by describing the animals that walk on the earth. They are not stupid animals; in their own way they are wise and cunning. The falcon with its superior eyesight and the lion with its superb hunting skill are both animals greatly admired. But animals, no matter how wise, do not and cannot grasp what is under the earth as they walk upon it. Even if people were to bring dazzling gems of great value for them to see, they would not have the capacity to begin to understand their value.

Job compares the precious metals and gems to God's wisdom and understanding. Although there is nothing of greater value, if we cannot *understand the value,* how can we discover and benefit from them?

I believe when God puts children in our homes, they are like the falcon and the lion. They don't understand what is of true value in life. The goal in maturing our children is to *mature their hearts* to the point that they can understand the value of God's wisdom and understanding. Only God can truly make your children "good." Only He can give you or your children the power to consistently resist temptation and live lives that are blessed by the fruit of good, godly behavior.

Summary: Chapter Eight

People who make decisions at Stage Five are motivated by a desire to follow the principles of life or self-evident truths that God has given to us in His word.

The ability to reach Stage Five thinking has been hampered in our society by some current cultural ideas:

- There is no absolute truth.

- Man is basically good (and therefore doesn't need God).

The best way to help people progress to Stage Five is to:

- Let your children watch you make decisions.

- Engage the culture as you sit, walk, and stand with your children.

To have a teenager who appreciates God's gifts of wisdom and understanding and can integrate those into his or her process of decision making is the ultimate achievement for a parent who desires a morally mature child.

CHAPTER 9

Stage Six—Where Truth and Love Meet

"Does it express ultimate love and respect?"

At this point in the journey you have gotten to the Mainland—Stages Five and Six on our path to good decision making. This is the *ultimate destination* for you and your children. There are no more bridges or tactics to promote growth. Now there is just a need to understand the new level of maturity and how to translate it into every area of life.

Stage Six is by far the most powerful place from which we can parent our children. I encourage you to find opportunities to practice operating from Stage Six as often as you can.

The Basis for Stage Six

Kohlberg was not always sure that a sixth stage existed, probably because there were very few people he could interview and observe for collection of data. For me, however, it was what I saw emerge as the sixth stage that convinced me that there was merit in the whole idea of stages of maturity.

The Secret Pathway the Heart Takes to Maturity takes a person from being motivated totally out of fear to being motivated totally out of love.

Fear ——————————————————————— Love

    (Fear and love are polar opposites.)

First John 4:18 says: "There is no fear in love. But perfect love drives out fear, because fear has to do with punishment. The one who fears is not made perfect in love."

The Bible also says, "The fear of the Lord is the beginning of wisdom" (Psalm 111:10).

Isn't it interesting that this verse places FEAR at the beginning of the development of wisdom? And that our journey to spiritual maturity that begins with fear ends with LOVE?

Stage Six is the point at which we can really begin to fulfill the greatest commandment of Scripture. Jesus said that all of the law and prophets could be summed up in this law: "'Love the Lord your God with all your heart and with all your soul and with all your mind" and "Love your neighbor as yourself'" (Matthew 22:37, 39). So the end result of the Scriptures or the full development of the Scriptures is that a person would love the Lord as well as his neighbor. Love of God and healthy love of others is the sum or the finished product of the moral development process.

WHAT STAGE SIX LOOKS LIKE

What does the sixth stage look like? Is it all birds and flowers and soft voices? Kohlberg himself acknowledged that if there were a Stage Six, then Jesus Christ was one of the few individuals to operate there. A close look at Jesus' life shows a love that can be worn in everyday situations. Not just a dress-up, look-good, Sunday-morning image, but a love that rolls with the punches and doesn't worry about image or self. Jesus was not trying to please people and make them comfortable. He was working toward their good, whether they appreciated Him or not. Since He did not fear their rejection of Him, He was able to love them even when they were in the process of humiliating and killing Him.

I saw a sign at a church once that said, "It is more important to do what is kind than to do what is right." Does that strike you as an odd thing to say? It certainly struck me that way! Kindness *should be* the right thing. However, true kindness may not always *look* compassionate to a world that loathes suffering of any kind.

For example, hell—eternal separation from God—does not look kind, but when God made us, He gave us the *freedom* to disobey Him; He doesn't force us to love and obey Him. The gift of freedom comes with built-in positive and negative effects. The most negative consequence is hell. Hell doesn't *look* kind, but it is very much an inseparable part of the magnificent gift—the gift of freedom—that God gave us. Earlier I shared about a time when I helped a baby chicken out of its shell. I thought I was being kind, but the results were disastrous! It takes mature thinking to be able to look deeper than the surface to determine what is kind and what is right.

So Stage Six is not all hearts and flowers. It is *real love in a real world*. Christ walked out that kind of daily love when He was on earth. He did things that may have seemed harsh at first glance, but a closer look confirms that He showed ultimate love in all circumstances.

Take, for example, the story of the rich young man (Matthew 19:16–22) who asked Jesus how he could receive eternal life. What a great opportunity for the young man—to be ministered to by the Son of God! When Jesus told him that he must obey the commandments, he quickly replied that he had done so. When he asked what more he had to do, Jesus told him he needed to sell all he had and give it to the poor, then come and follow Him. The man was instantly sad because he was very wealthy. And amazingly Jesus let him walk away!

No doubt Jesus loved that young man, but He knew his heart needed to hear the brutal truth. Jesus knew that the man's possessions were his prison bars, and he was seeking to obtain eternal life on top of everything else he possessed. He was not looking to be saved; at that point he didn't know he *needed* to be saved. The bounty of his possessions hid his most dire need even from himself. Jesus knew the best chance for him to understand his need to be saved was for him to get a good glimpse at his own priorities—which I'm sure he did as he sorrowfully walked away.

In short, the Sixth Stage starts with the belief that truth and love always meet. They are like two ladders that eventually cross paths. Sometimes we must climb pretty far up the ladders before we can find the place where they intersect. It takes complex thinking skills. But once a person knows the two ladders will always cross, it becomes a matter of determination and perseverance to see it happen.

Living the Christian life often presents a dilemma. *How do we love sinners without seeming to endorse their sin?* This is a huge question for Christians today. I believe the answer is in understanding this stage of moral maturity.

Stage Six is where a person understands that pure truth cannot be separated from love. Truth without love is a "resounding gong or a clanging cymbal" (1 Corinthians 13:1), while love without truth is dysfunction!

In the story of Helen Keller I love the role Anne Sullivan played in Helen's life. It serves as a great example of Stage Six leadership. Anne was a young girl who had just graduated from blind school when she was asked to live and work with seven-year-old Helen Keller. Anne herself was half blind and had no family to care for her, so she was thankful to get the job.

From the very beginning Anne began to set down boundaries for Helen, and Helen did not like boundaries. Not having the ability to see or hear, she had only the crudest skills for manipulating her environment. She hit, scratched, and attacked like an animal when she was not given her way. She disrupted the entire household when she pleased, helping herself to everyone's plate at the table, and she needed constant care. Her parents' goals for Helen were simple: They wanted a quiet, demure child who could eat at the table and fold her napkin. But Anne Sullivan realized right away that Helen had the potential to go far beyond her parents' expectations.

In order for Anne to help Helen get to a place where she was teachable, Anne had to work intensely with her, and Helen resented being forced to accommodate herself to Anne's agenda. Helen fought hard, one time even knocking out one of Anne's teeth. But she continued to work with Helen with the intent to enable her to reach her greatest potential. Initially Helen's parents were not supportive of Anne's methods, so Anne found herself laying her job on the line as she insisted that she needed *more* freedom with Helen, not less, to accomplish her goals for the young girl.

Although she was still a fairly young woman herself, Anne

was not afraid of Helen or Helen's parents. She was passionate about the potential she saw in Helen, and that carried her through the rough times. She didn't get frustrated and give up on Helen when Helen hurt her. She didn't get angry and decide to let Mr. and Mrs. Keller "get what they deserved" and just quit! She let her love of Helen and her desire for the truth of Helen's full potential keep her at her post.

That story is a great illustration for parents. So many times our children do not appreciate the boundaries or discipline we put on them. We need to be big-hearted toward them and realize that from their current perspective they may not be able to grasp how beneficial our decisions are for their future. Fix your eyes on their future and take heart. Don't be afraid of their disapproval. If you do change your mind on a decision, *don't change it out of fear!* Change your mind only because you have somehow become convinced it is in your child's best interest to do so.

I am terribly aware that when all is said and done, neither my husband nor I will stand before our *children* to give an account for how we raised them. It will be before *God* that we stand, and so God is the only one we should fear.

How Is Stage Six Different From Stage Five?

If all principles are rooted in love, how different can Stage Six be from Stage Five?

This is a great question. Is there enough of a distinction between the last two stages to warrant giving Stage Six a chapter in this book? I would say an emphatic yes!

• Laws are *understood* at Stage Four.

- *Good* laws come from *life principles,* and life principles are understood at Stage Five.

- Good principles come from the two great characteristics that describe God: love and holiness (or truth).

It does seem a bit backward, doesn't it? Perhaps the reason the development stages are in this order is because people can understand laws more easily than they can principles. Laws are less complex than principles. Principles are higher laws that sit above circumstances. Laws are pre-digested, circumstance-driven rules.

Principles are harder to teach than laws or rules. Parents who teach principles have to think harder and must teach their children throughout the day as they encounter different situations. Thinking in principles requires a higher level of reasoning skills. So teaching a teenager to think at this higher level can be a big job, but the hard work is worth it!

It's incredibly important that parents take the challenge and put the effort into maturing their teens to the highest level of moral development possible. If there are not enough people in our societies who are able to think at this level, our world will lose something extremely valuable. Remember, the Bible is written in Stage Five thought (principles that need to be interpreted and applied to life). If our teenagers can only think and live at Stage Three, they can't even *understand* biblical thinking.

CHECK YOUR MOTIVES

What stage are you currently working at with your children? What motivates you in the everyday decisions you make regarding your children and your home?

Ask yourself: Do these thoughts go through my mind as I make decisions?

- If I do that, my kids will hate me!

- If I do that, my life will be filled with conflict!

- If I am not careful, my kids will embarrass me!

- My teenagers don't want to spend time with me at this stage of their lives, so I will pull away from them like they are pulling away from me. Serves them right!

- As a parent I would hate to be seen as a failure.

- Nobody has a good relationship with his or her teenager. Why should I expect to?

All of these thoughts can be tied to a motive found at Stages One through Four. All of these thoughts have threads of fear throughout them.

Consider the greater motive that Stage Six offers. Here parents sincerely seek to honor God in their parenting. All of us as parents are asked to basically make the same sacrifice Abraham had to make. Not literally, of course, but God does ask us to put Him first, even before our children. He knows that putting our kids first would be to everyone's detriment. Stage Six parents have only one fear—a healthy fear of God. They fear displeasing Him more than they fear any scenario with their children.

Parents operating at Stage Six consider their child's future and protect him or her even when such tender care is not appreciated. Going back to the illustration of the gerbil I kept in my classroom, I knew all the dangers that were out in the big bad classroom (about twenty little hands that had not been trained how to grasp a gerbil without squeezing the life out of it). The gerbil was completely unaware of the dangers, however, and really resented my efforts to keep him in his cage. As a parent, you must make sure that your motives are for your child's best interest, even if it's years before he or she can begin to be thankful for your efforts.

The Example of Christ

The story of Jesus Christ is a powerful illustration of sixth-stage leadership.

Christ is GOD. He was the One who created the universe, the Word that made light and plants, earth and stars. He made all the spinning galaxies and He understands all the mysteries of life.

Then He became a man. I've often thought that Christ becoming a man had to be the most difficult miracle ever performed. He became one of us. He got hungry, tired, and thirsty.

Because of the message He was sent to give, and just the fact of who He was, certain people hated Him. They plotted to kill Him. And He let them live.

One night, the people who hated Him captured Him and put Him in a room with high-ranking officials who began a series of steps that would result in His death. The high-ranking officials sent Him out and ordered that He be beaten. Then the common soldiers were brought in. It was their turn with Him. The lowliest of soldiers mocked Him. They put a purple robe on Him as a joke and put a crown of thorns on His head. Although He'd already received a professional beating, they struck Him with a stick and spit on Him. They pretended to worship Him.

Then they force-marched Him up a hill, stripped Him of His clothes, and nailed His hands and feet to a cross—a common death instrument for criminals.

What was Christ's response?

> *"Father, forgive them, for they do not know what they are doing"* (Luke 23:34).

How could Jesus have that attitude at such an intense moment? I believe His attitude was the same one we find in the gospel of John, right before Jesus washed the disciples' feet.

> *Jesus knew that the Father had put all things under his power, and that he had come from God and was returning to God.* (John 13:3)

That is the same attitude we need to arrive at as we seek to be Stage Six parents. God will give us all we need to do what He asks us to do. It was His decision to place you as the father or mother in your family, so you can be confident in the role He has given you to fill. A screaming toddler or a turbulent teenager should not be able to shake you, because your confidence is rooted not in your own strength but in the fact that *God chose you for the job* and His plans can be trusted.

STAGE SIX THINKING IN CRISIS MOMENTS

It is most important to remember Stage Six when life gets tense—that's when Stage Six shines the brightest. Relationship situations sometimes get pretty intense. I remember well the tough situation I faced when I worked on staff in charge of the children's ministry at a church. I had to "fire" a volunteer who worked with the children because she was living with her boyfriend. I don't know about your church, but that's not okay in my church.

However, I didn't want to just get her off my staff; I really wanted to *minister* to her. But how does one minister to someone while "firing" her?

I asked her to meet me in my office, and I started out by confirming that she really was living with her boyfriend. I then told her that while I cared deeply about putting the right teachers in the right classes, I also cared deeply about her and her walk with God. I encouraged her to tell me about her hopes and dreams for the future. She shared a desire to be a wife and mother of a healthy family. I affirmed her desire and then told her that I wanted to help her get to her destination by walking with her through a set of difficult decisions she was going to have to make in order to get back on the right track.

I wasn't sure she would be willing to make the tough decisions, but she did. She ended up moving out of her boyfriend's apartment. They postponed the original date for their wedding, went to marriage counseling, and later that year got married.

Did I "fire" a volunteer who was living in sin? Yes. Did I use the circumstance as an opportunity to communicate God's love for her ultimate good? Yes!

That's what we must be motivated to do as parents. Deal with the truth of the situation, or the sin, but also look for the opportunity to express God's perspective and love within the situation.

If your wife or husband said they loved you every day

for five years and then randomly one day, in the heat of emotion, told you they hated you, which message would you believe? It is likely that you would disregard five years of the faithful message and fixate on the message communicated in one passionate moment. That's often what happens in families.

Stage Six parenting is meant for every day, but it becomes even more powerful when children see love and truth wielded together in the intense crisis moments of life. It's an opportunity to convey a powerful message that common, ordinary days don't offer.

STAGE SIX IN EVERYDAY SITUATIONS

Although it is powerful to engage in Stage Six thinking during a crisis moment, it's really convenient for successfully resolving everyday situations as well. When a child is being verbally disrespectful, it is a good time to practice climbing the truth and love ladders. Although it is normal to recoil when being verbally attacked, a Stage Six parent who is operating with no fear can calmly model servant leadership.

For example, the parent can say, "I don't care if you talk to me that way. It's not about me. What I *do* care about is if I let you talk to me this way, you will eventually talk to your boss the same way, and that can negatively affect your future career. I also know if I let you talk to me this way, it will eventually affect how you talk to your wife (or husband) and children, and that can negatively affect your future family. So you see, I can't let you talk to me this way and still get a good grade as a parent. I really want to do what is right by you and give you the best opportunity possible for a bright future."

I encourage you to use Stage Six problem solving whether

you are dealing with a full-blown crisis or a nagging everyday problem.

Every week I am challenged to make decisions differently now that I know about Stage Six. One of the ways I sleuth out my true motive is to search for any trace of fear.

- What am I afraid of in this situation?

- Do I fear anything or anyone more than God in this issue?

- Am I handling both love and truth as an inseparable unit?

- What is the real truth regarding this problem? How does God see it?

- What do I love about the person I am dealing with? What makes me care about this problem? (Their character, their connection with God, their future, etc.)

Just these simple questions have helped me encourage people in counseling situations. If people have an impending confrontation, it helps for them to sleuth out all the fear in the situation, then to let go of any fear except the fear of displeasing God. When we're able to replace the fear with godly love for the people involved, the situation becomes completely different. Interestingly, it usually loses the sense of confrontation that hovered over it before.

Does Stage Six exist? Absolutely. We know it does because God compels us in His word to attain to it. Stage Six not only exists, but it is the stage from which anyone who seeks any kind of leadership, whether it's church leadership, parenting, or being a corporate CEO, should operate. Stage Six exemplifies servant leadership.

THE ATTITUDE OF STAGE SIX PARENTS

A mom told me a story once that has helped me better communicate the attitude of parents operating at this stage of moral development. She told me her oldest son had been a fairly compliant child, but one day when he was ten years old, he apparently decided he was tired of being obedient. At this particular time of his life she was homeschooling him. Her husband traveled a lot, and homeschooling allowed the family to travel with him at times.

On this particular day it was close to lunchtime when the mother told her son she wanted him to leave what he was doing and come sit at the table to take a spelling test. After he took the test, she explained, they would eat lunch. The boy was absorbed in another activity and did not respond. She gently approached him again, at which time he looked at her with defiance and said, no—he wouldn't take the test. "And you can't make me!"

The mom was shocked because the boy had never acted that way before. What should her response be, she wondered? She decided it would be best to handle the situation calmly, so she reasoned with him. "Right now I am not speaking to you as Mom; I am speaking to you as your teacher. Get up and go to the table for your spelling test."

The boy dug in stubbornly. "No, I won't do it and you can't make me!"

The mom was desperate, trying to think quickly of something to do. "Okay, I guess I will just have to call the principal." She'd never called her husband the principal before, but for some reason her son knew exactly what she meant. He watched with great interest as she went to the phone and called her husband.

When he answered the phone she calmly informed him who she was (as if he didn't know!), then she explained she had a student who was unwilling to obey. There was a pause as she listened to his response. She said okay and then hung up.

The boy curiously watched it all and was greatly relieved when his mother hung up the phone and went back into the kitchen.

Although her husband traveled a lot, on this particular day he was at his office in town, which was only three minutes from their house. In three minutes the son heard a noise in front of the house, and the father, a very tall man, walked through the front door. The boy froze where he was. He hadn't forecasted anything like *that* happening! The father calmly walked over to his son and stood straight over him, his large frame casting quite a shadow on his young, frightened boy.

"Son, your mother tells me you are refusing to get up and go to the table to take a test. Is this true?"

The son silently nodded his agreement, looking up at his dad with wide eyes.

"She also says you told her she couldn't make you. Is this true?"

Again the boy nodded silently, but this time his lower lip was trembling.

The father then knelt down beside the boy and drew him into his arms and softly said, "How can I help?"

The boy began to cry, and his father comforted him. Shortly thereafter he got up, dried his tears, and sat at the table for his spelling test. The mother related to me that never in her whole life had she loved her husband as much as she loved him at that moment.

I'm sure many of you wish your parenting problems could be so simply resolved, but the deciding factor in that situation was the father's attitude—it was a perfect six. And the good news is that this attitude—*How can I help?*—can work in any situation!

Whether your child is three and throwing a tantrum or fifteen and having a volcano moment, the "How can I help?" attitude will serve you well.

Sure, the kind of help they *want* at the moment is to get their way, but the kind of help they *need* is to learn important life lessons and skills so they can acquire wisdom and grow in favor with God and man. The "How can I help?" attitude is all about giving your children what they *need*.

Summary: Chapter Nine

The motive behind Stage Six decisions is a blend of love and truth.

Love and truth always intersect. But in complex circumstances, like determining how to love the sinner without endorsing the sin, it is difficult to see *how* they intersect.

The importance of working with both truth and love is:

- Truth without love is a "resounding gong" and "clanging cymbal" (1 Corinthians 13:1).

- Love without truth is not love—it's dysfunction! (1 Corinthians 13:6)

Check your motives. . . . Are they operating at Stage Six?

- What am I afraid of in this situation?

- Do I fear anything or anyone more than God with this issue?

- Am I handling both truth and love as an inseparable unit?

- What is the real truth regarding this problem? How does God see it?

- What do I love about the person I am dealing with? What makes me care about this problem? (Their character, their connection with God, their future, etc.)

The Stage Six Attitude:

How can I help? (Giving your children what they need, not necessarily what they want)

CHAPTER 10

Level Three— It's Bigger Than Us!

The ultimate destination in moral maturity is all about the discovery that we are not alone in our fate. There is a God, He made us, He cares about us, and He should be actively considered in our decisions. This is a huge leap for someone steeped in modern culture. The culture may (for the moment) support that there is a God, as in "One nation under God," but generally it doesn't support the idea that there is a God who is *active* in our lives. This is why the origins of man can be such a conflict-ridden topic. To embrace the idea that God created us means that we belong to Him. And if that's true, He's responsible for us and *we should obey Him*.

The kinds of things that mark the ultimate destination for our heart's maturity—principles, love, respect, and truth—tell us a lot about the character of God. God is perfect in every way, including His character. And of all the character traits that describe Him, the two that rise to the top are always *love* and *holiness*. Our highest response back to God is to reflect His character traits in our lives.

However, God's ways are above our ways. How can we possibly understand enough to be able to reflect His character? God knows our human weaknesses. He knows we start out with very little understanding of Him, devoid of true wisdom. He knows that we start out with primal fear motivating us, but His goal is to mature us to a place where we value and understand His love and truth (holiness). It's a long trip for us; that's why it's a lifelong journey.

Some psychologists say there are only two root emotions: love and fear. The Secret Path the Heart Takes to Maturity begins at the most primal and immature response—fear. And it ends up at the highest and most mature response—love. It is a progression that God reveals in His word. God's story, the Bible, is a story of God working with mankind, developing maturity in us over time. His overall plan can be seen as we look back over the hilltops of biblical times.

God's Unfolding Revelation to Us

- God worked with Adam and Eve in Stage One (Fear of Punishment) when He told them not to eat of the forbidden fruit or they would die.

- Eve sinned in Stage Two (Anticipation of Reward) when she took the fruit because it was desirable to her.

- God worked with Abraham in Stage Two when He continually promised him blessings. (I will bless you, I will bless you, I will bless you!)

- God then bound Abraham's descendants together as a

nation, setting them apart and promising them a home-land. They became a nation of people who belonged together, sharing special traditions and a unique history. It was as if they all belonged to a very exclusive club.

STAGE THREE—CRUDE CONFORMITY

Did you ever wonder why God did that? Why He made the Israelites into such an exclusive nation? It was to meet the developmental needs of a nation, the *need to belong*. It was also at this point that regular blood sacrifices were offered. Mankind needed God's grace before they could understand it. So God established the practice of animal sacrifice. Were the sacrifices for God or were they for us? They were for us. We *needed* grace before we could *understand* grace.

Then God gave the Israelites the Law. Most of it was geared to a Stage Four understanding as God continued to mature them in their moral development. While the Law was an important part of the journey God wanted us to take, He wants all of us to mature *beyond* the Law. Jesus alludes to this in Matthew 9:13 when He quotes from Hosea 6:6: "'I desire mercy, not sacrifice.'" God knew we needed to understand at a law level *before* we could comprehend the higher level of principles.

Have you ever wondered why God gave the Law only to pronounce it ineffective later? (See Hebrews 9.) The third chapter of Galatians describes how the Law was designed to bring us to Christ (in order to mature us). God was maturing the hearts of the Israelites to be able to understand and accept Christ as much as possible. That is why when He came, Christ told the Jewish people, "'Do not think that I have come to abolish the Law or the Prophets; I have not come to abolish them but to fulfill them'" (Matthew 5:17).

Then God sent Jesus—the Word—to us. Christ modeled and taught Stage Five principles throughout His life. While the Old Testament laws focused on outward behaviors, Jesus taught about deeper issues such as attitude and motive—principles that transcend any culture or era.

Then Jesus, stretching our minds even further to Stage Six thinking, said:

> "Love the Lord your God with all your heart and with all your soul and with all your mind." This is the first and greatest commandment. And the second is like it: "Love your neighbor as yourself." All the Law and the Prophets hang on these two commandments. (Matthew 22:37–40)

Summary: Chapter Ten

Level Three (which includes Stages Five and Six) completes the motivation journey from fear to love.

God desires for us to be mature, but He knows that His ways are "higher than" our ways (Isaiah 55:9), so He works carefully with us to develop us stage by stage. His final goal is to bring us to maturity in Christ.

The Bible is God's story of the secret path the human heart takes to reach moral maturity.

Some ways God worked with mankind in the Old Testament to prepare them for Christ:

- He motivated them with punishment in the Garden. (Stage One)

- He motivated Abraham with blessings (or rewards) as He developed a relationship with him. (Stage Two)

- He developed a nation whose members felt a strong sense of belonging. (Stage Three)

- He established animal sacrifice so people could tangibly experience His grace—a very complex concept. (Stage Three)

- He gave the Law to His people. (Stage Four)

- He fulfilled the purpose of the Law by sending Christ, who taught in interpretive principles—parables and object lessons. (Stage Five)

- Christ then tells us that the end goal of God's dealings with mankind is that we are to love Him and love others. (Stage Six)

CHAPTER 11

Practical Tips: Making It Work

Working as a volunteer on a church building project, I was hammering nails as I had been told. It was hard work. When the contractor in charge mentioned to me that he was tempted to cut the handle off my hammer, I looked at him like he was crazy. "What would you do that for?" I asked.

He explained that I didn't need the handle. Then I looked at my hand and realized what he meant: I was holding the hammer by the neck. No wonder it was such hard work driving those nails!

Like a good hammer, the material in this book is supposed to be a tool to make your job as a parent easier. If you have arrived here honestly (not skipping any of the material in the first ten chapters), you've read through lots of detail about the secret path the heart takes to maturity. In this chapter I want to look at how you can use this tool as effectively as possible.

There are several different ways to use this tool to help your children (or you) grow in maturity. The first is simple.

You've got to "get it"—understand that motives are more important than behavior in the long run. While it's nice to have obedient children, it's even more important that you understand *why* they are obeying!

Start With Yourself

There are several ways to use the Secret Path to Heart Maturity system in your everyday life. And the best way to start is to use the tool to examine your own motives.

You will find that you don't operate consistently at the same stage at all times, so don't try to "peg" yourself. Just try to honestly assess what stage you are operating at in the various areas of your life.

You might catch yourself disciplining your children in Stage Three, worried about what others are thinking of you as a parent. Are you worried about appearances to the point that it affects your decisions?

In another area you might find yourself being motivated by Stage Four. For example, as you listen to the news, do you find yourself pulled into the orbit of public opinion without critically thinking about the issues? Do you have relationships that are manipulative—where either you are manipulating others or you are being manipulated by them? Do you find yourself fearing people, or wanting to control situations more than seeking to discover what God wants you to do, say, or think? Those kinds of thoughts are generated at the lower stages of moral maturity.

Think back to your childhood. Do you remember what it felt like to make decisions out of fear? Do you remember being motivated by rewards? Do you remember feeling a deep need to be accepted—and finding yourself doing things that you hoped would guarantee acceptance by your family or the crowd?

If you are a Christian, ask yourself at what stage you came to Christ. People come to Christ at different stages. Here are some common ways:

Stage One—Fear of Hell
Stage Two—Anticipation of Heaven
Stage Three—Wanting God's Love and Acceptance
Stage Four is more complex to describe. Your decision to accept Christ could have been based on your understanding of the rules of the church rather than God's laws (e.g., joining the church, becoming a member).

Assessing where you are and where you've operated in the past is a good start as you prepare to move forward with your family.

Discuss Moral Development Regularly

Maturity increases when it is discussed and valued. Talk about the importance motives play in decision making with your children. Encourage them to see the immaturity of the lower stages of moral development. Make it a game to peg your decisions as you make them.

Once I was hoping to encourage my fifteen-year-old daughter to do an extra task for me. I promised her what I thought was a great reward, but her face told me she wasn't buying it. She said, "Mom, you're dealing with me at Stage Two. How immature do you think I am?" She then did the task *for nothing*. Imagine that! Just by talking about motives and higher stages of maturity, my three teenagers have changed the way they make decisions. It has raised their level of moral maturity.

Interestingly, Lawrence Kohlberg did not believe humans could raise their level of maturity. He believed we are just like animals, on a developmental path that cannot be altered. He saw man as nothing more than a smart animal. But Kohlberg's own research proved him wrong on this point.

He set up weekly discussion groups in which the people discussed moral development and applied it to their lives. Kohlberg's own records showed that the participants *increased in maturity* simply by talking about it!

Try it in your own family. Make it a game. Let's say you're all on your way to an older couple's house. As a parent, you want to encourage your kids to be on their best behavior while they visit there. Before you arrive, have your kids guess which stage you're working at as you say these things:

> You better behave when we get to the Smiths or you'll be punished! (Stage One)
>
> If you all behave really well, we'll go out for ice cream on the way home! (Stage Two)
>
> You better not embarrass us in front of the Smiths tonight! (Stage Three)
>
> Don't misbehave—the Smiths will think you're hooligans! (Stage Three)
>
> Okay, let's talk about how we should behave tonight at the Smiths' house: What kind of things should we all remember to do or not do? (Stage Four)
>
> The Smiths are older people and maybe they're not used to children in their home. The Bible tells us we need to honor them and treat them with respect. How can we do that tonight? (Stage Five)

The Smiths are such precious people. God loves them. How can we show love to them tonight while we visit them in their home? (Stage Six)

Talking to your children about the maturity process will not only help them see what their motivation levels are but will also help them to assess the motivational levels of *others*. Once, after I'd given a talk to a singles group, a young woman told me a heartbreaking story. She had made the commitment when she was a girl to stay sexually pure and had kept her commitment all through high school and six years of college. Then, when she was in her late twenties, she dated a man who pushed her boundaries. She refused his advances and remained strong for several months, but she finally gave in. Soon after, the relationship ended and she was left with deep regret.

As she listened to the characteristics of the first four stages, she realized that her boyfriend had pressured her at every stage. He threatened her at Stage One. He promised her the moon in Stage Two. He shamed her in Stage Three. And he reasoned with her in Stage Four. Before she left that night she remarked sadly to me that if she had known about the different stages of motivation, she would have recognized her boyfriend's low level of reasoning and would not have succumbed to his pressuring tactics. Just talking about the motives behind decisions can help protect your children from being trapped by the foolish reasoning of the world.

Teach and Model Principles

I hope in reading this book you are inspired to teach principles to your children. I know this was already discussed in chapter 8, where we dealt with Stage Five motivation, but let me say it again: The greatest way to encourage your child to develop into a principled thinker is to consistently teach principles and model them through everyday life. Parents can get lost in teaching rules: Don't lose your jacket; clean your room; be nice to your sister. We can get so busy sculpting outward behavior that we forget to tell our kids *why* certain behaviors are right or wrong.

There are two basic ways to teach principles. One way is to integrate them into the everyday concerns of family life. As jackets get lost, as rooms beg to be cleaned, and as sisters need to be treated with respect, grab the everyday opportunities to teach principles. Ask your children: What is the deepest *reason* for not losing our jackets, cleaning our rooms, or being nice to our sisters?

Another way to teach principles is to intentionally make it part of your day's schedule. As you read Bible stories to small children, discuss principles along with the biblical events. As you take the time to pray with your teenagers, find ways to also teach life principles in the process.

A biblically based character education curriculum can be a great tool to use. The best character education materials I have found can be viewed on the Internet at *www.characterfirst. com*. Take the time and be deliberate about teaching and modeling God's principles. Remember, the world's system has time and a definite agenda for the young man or woman in your home.

On a motivational level it is important to understand where your child is *operating* so you can make sure you are providing what he or she needs for that stage. Remember the handrails that will help your children across to the next stage of development; don't let them camp out indefinitely at a lower level of motivation. Thankfully, once they are able to think at the principle level, their motivation will come from their own convictions, not from you. And that's a worthy goal to shoot for!

Teach and Model a Dynamic Relationship With God

We help our children develop morally when we teach them about God's desire to have a relationship with them and introduce them to Him as their heavenly Father. God designed us to be able to grow into a greater understanding of who He is. This in turn enables Him to work more intricately in our lives. As our relationship with Him deepens and we walk in more intimacy with Him, He is able to bring more and more maturity to our hearts.

Keep in mind that *God deeply desires for your children to mature.* He wants to work with your children the way He worked with Joseph and David in the Old Testament. Your children need to know God and develop a relationship with Him so that He can actively work with them throughout their lives.

THE POWER OF PARENTS

I have especially targeted this book for the benefit of parents because they are the only people group who have *real power* to raise the moral development of the next generation. It almost seems as if society would like you to feel powerless, but the last twenty years of research on the subject of parental influence shows otherwise. Parents are the greatest *persons of influence* in a child's life. And this even includes teenagers!

Have you noticed how anti-smoking, anti-drug, and anti-promiscuous-sex advertisements have changed? The ads used to appeal directly to the teenager through motivations from Stages One, Two, and Three: Don't do drugs; you'll hurt yourself or someone you love. Don't smoke; it's not cool.

But now the ads directly appeal to the parents: Parents, talk to your kids about smoking. Parents, talk to your kids about drugs. Parents, talk to your kids about sex.

Twenty years of research has piled up at the dock of our culture, and the findings have become too overwhelming to ignore. Parents are the most influential people (for bad or good) in their child's life, whether the child is three or seventeen.

If moral development rises in the world it will be because of the influence of parents. *If the Ten Commandments get chiseled onto the most important monument in the country—our children's hearts—it will be because parents like you were brave and intentional.*

Summary: Chapter Eleven

The six stages of The Secret Path the Heart Takes to Maturity are a tool, a means of helping parents guide their children in moral development. To use the tool most effectively, there are some important things to remember:

- Give weight to the importance of motives.

- Examine your own motives.

- Discuss the stages of moral development regularly as a family.

- Teach and model biblical principles.

- Teach your children about and *model* a relationship with God.

- Recognize and use wisely the tremendous power you have as a parent.

Play the Game Well . . .

Parenting is like a game. Not in terms of significance—but as far as end-goal success, parenting can be compared to playing a game. It's not like chess, which requires ALL skill and no luck, but neither is it a game like Candy Land, a game that depends completely on the roll of the dice. No . . . parenting is like backgammon, a game that requires a *mixture* of skill and luck, or, to be more accurate in respect to parenting, a mixture of skill and *free will.*

Although as parents we cannot completely control or guarantee our child's decision to value God's truths and become mature, we can hone our skills at parenting and powerfully up our odds in the game.

It is my prayer that you are able to take the principles and tools in this book and use them to further increase your influence, sharpen your skills, and greatly advance your odds of maturing *Stage Six* leaders for tomorrow. Leaders who will bless you most by becoming great parents for your grandchildren!

Study Guide

Chapter One: Study Questions
The Secret Path the Heart Takes to Maturity
(A Case for Considering Inner Motives)

God's Word clearly communicates God's expectations regarding our outward behavior. As a result, we often see only outward behavior as that which is pleasing or not pleasing to God.

Read the following verses and note what God's word says He *truly* values most in us.

Psalm 51:16–17 _____

Hebrews 11:6 _____

Psalm 69:30–31 _____

Psalm 51:6 _____

Look at the list you just made. Are these "items" you can just check off as "done"?

Why is it harder to check off a list that's based on heart issues than it is to check off a list of outward behaviors such as Jesus quoted to the rich young man in Mark 10:19? "Do not murder, do not commit adultery, do not steal, do not give false testimony, do not defraud, honor your father and mother."

_____

_____

What is humanly attractive about fulfilling a list of outward behaviors rather than grappling with the deeper issues of the heart?

_____

_____

In which situation do we need to be more dependent on God: Avoiding a list of outward behaviors or keeping our thoughts, motives, and attitudes pleasing to God?

_____

_____

Chapter Two: Study Questions
The Island of Fear

In a healthy environment, kids know what the boundaries are. They know what is expected of them and what they must avoid to escape punishment.

Read Deuteronomy 11:13–32. God sets before the children of Israel a blessing and a curse. How were they to obtain the blessing and avoid the curse?

_____

God has clearly defined the boundaries. Have you clearly defined the boundaries in your home?

Read Deuteronomy 5:7–21. How is each of the Ten Commandments more about *freedom* than *restriction*? (Hint: what kind of world would you live in if there were no consequences or stigmas for breaking each of the commandments?)

No other gods

No idol worship

Don't use God's name in vain

Keep the Sabbath

Honor your father and mother

Do not murder

Do not commit adultery

Do not steal

_____

Do not bear false witness

_____

Do not covet

_____

What ways could you communicate the freedom aspect along with the punishment aspect as you enforce the boundaries in your home?

_____

_____

Chapter Three: Study Questions
The Island of Reward

As we mature, it is not that our desire for reward goes completely away; it just gets anchored in the right place.

Read Hebrews 11:6. How important is the reward connection to our faith?

_____

_____

Read Matthew 5:3–11 and note the rewards that are promised for each attitude.

Attitude:	Reward:
(example) Poor in spirit	*(example) Kingdom of Heaven*
_____	_____
_____	_____
_____	_____
_____	_____
_____	

In Philippians 3:14, Paul was motivated by what reward?

_____

The concept of rewards being linked to pleasing God is an important part of our faith. Does this put a different emphasis (different than just behavior control) on how you view rewards in your home?

_____

What ways can you teach your child about God's character through the giving of appropriate rewards?

_____

_____

Chapter Four: Study Questions
It's All About Me!

People stuck at Level One tend to think everyone else is out for "number one" just like they are.

Take a look at the two thieves on the cross. (Luke 23:39–42)

Which thief is at Level One in understanding?

_____

Which thief displays an understanding of the Law?

_____

What is it that he knows about the Law?

_____

Which thief displays an understanding of his need for God's grace?

_____

What is it that he knows about grace?

_____

What is the greatest tragedy about the Level One thief's lack of understanding?

_____

How does our society's becoming more and more "me centered" impact our effectiveness in sharing the Gospel?

_____

_____

What people group in society is most able to move the culture forward—beyond "me centeredness"?

_____

(Hint: You're reading a *parenting* book!)

Chapter Five: Study Questions
The Island of Crude Conformity

Read Acts 5:1–11. In verse 4 Ananias's motive is questioned. In that light, what do you think the motive was behind his giving? (See also Acts 2:44–45)

Whose approval was Ananias seeking?

Contrast that story with the story of Zacchaeus. (Luke 19:1–10)

What do you think the motive was behind his giving?

The men were similar in their outward generosity but differed greatly in their inner motive. Many of the loving behaviors the Bible compels us to do *can* be done with the desire to please people. In light of these two stories, how important is it to God for our motive to be pleasing *Him* rather than *them*?

In what areas of your life are you most tempted to please people over God? (church, work, friends, family)

What are some ways you can check yourself and reorient your motives in these areas?

Chapter Six: Study Questions
The Island of Majority Rules

Jesus said He did not come to abolish the Law but to fulfill it. Whereas we might think that the Law is an end unto itself, Christ showed us that the Law's purpose was to start us on a path to understanding the principles of truth and grace.

Read Matthew 5:17–48. There are two repeating phrases: "You have heard that it was said" and "But I tell you." Write the old law ("You have heard that it was said") under the Then column and write the new principle ("But I tell you") under the Now column.

Then: Now:

(example) Vs. 21 Do not murder   *(example) Be careful with your anger and harsh words*

_____   _____

_____   _____

_____   _____

How do these verses help you understand Christ's statement below?

_____

_____

"Do not think that I have come to abolish the Law or the Prophets; I have not come to abolish them but to fulfill them." (Matthew 5:17)

The Law has to do with outward behavior. But God operates at a deeper heart level. In what areas of life do you find yourself focusing on your own or others' outward behaviors rather than the deeper heart issues? (Judging others, your own successes or failures, etc.)

_____

_____

_____

What would be an action or plan you could implement in your life to better focus on heart issues instead of outward behaviors?

_____

_____

_____

How can you communicate this deeper understanding as you talk with your children in different life circumstances?

_____

_____

Chapter Seven: Study Questions
It's All About Us!

Levels One and Two are both dangerous plateaus on which to linger very long. The danger is that neither of them involves

God directly in decision making. Godly decisions may be made if a person is in a Christian family or theocratic society. But *true maturity* is when *God is integrated directly* into our decision making process.

Read the following examples of people who made decisions without the Lord's input:

Chronicles 13:1–16:14
Joshua 9
1 Chronicles 21:1–17
Acts 19:13–16
Numbers 13:26–29; 14:23–24

Does God want to be part of our everyday decisions? (Proverbs 3:5–6)

_____

As children get older it becomes essential that parents model good decision making. What are ways you can show your children how you seek God's will before making decisions?

_____

_____

Chapter Eight: Study Questions
Self-Evident Truths

Sometimes, even though we know and understand the basic principles of the Bible, it's hard to implement them into the various circumstances of our lives. Sometimes we're too close to an emotional situation to see clearly, sometimes we're

afraid, and sometimes we are just plain tired and aren't thinking.

Read the fourth chapter of Esther.

Mordecai told Esther to do something extremely irrational
and dangerous. King Xerxes was a tyrant who was completely
unpredictable. What was Esther's reason for not complying
with Mordecai's request? (v. 11)

_____

_____

As Mordecai continues to persuade Esther, he gives her two
good reasons why she should do as he has asked. What are
those two reasons?

1. (v. 13)

_____

_____

2. (v. 14b)

_____

_____

Mordecai's first argument is simply good human logic. His
second argument stems from a principle derived from what
we know about the character of God. How does bringing in
the aspect of God's sovereignty help Esther move forward?

_____

_____

_____

Think of a complex situation or difficult relationship you are dealing with. How might a biblical principle help you cope, function, or solve the problem?

_____

_____

_____

What kinds of things *inhibit you* from making principled-thinking decisions in your day-to-day or crisis situations?

_____

_____

_____

How might having a Mordecai—someone outside of the situation who has wisdom—help in certain circumstances?

_____

_____

Chapter Nine: Study Questions
Where Truth and Love Meet

Stage Six is a place where love and truth come together. The hardest time to think in Stage Six is usually when there is a need for confrontation.

First Corinthians 5:1–12 details Paul's instructions to break fellowship with a sexually immoral brother.

According to Paul, what should the church do in cases of sexual immorality?

_____

_____

What is the attitude behind the punishment? (v. 2)

_____

What is the purpose of the punishment? (v. 5)

_____

Why are we supposed to judge the people in the church but not outside the church? (vs. 12–13)

_____

Read 2 Corinthians 2:5–11 to see Paul's response to another circumstance in which a brother was punished and then repented.

Many times in confrontation we see the person we are confronting as the enemy. Who does Paul define as the real enemy? (v. 11)

_____

How might keeping your child's true best interest in mind help you in confrontational or disciplinary situations? (Ephesians 6:4; Colossians 3:21)

_____

_____

Chapter Ten: Study Questions
It's Bigger Than Us!

Level Three is a place where God, His Spirit, and His Word are our decision-making map. God deserves this power in our lives because He is ruler of all things.

Read the following verses and note what God is in charge of:

Romans 13:1

_____

Romans 9:20–21

_____

Luke 12:25–31

_____

Deuteronomy 8:17–18

_____

Romans 6:23

_____

Psalm 127

_____

Psalm 104

_____

In what areas of life do you tend to think that God is not interested?

How can you integrate God deeper into that area of your life?

Chapter Eleven: Study Questions
Practical Tips: Making It Work

Matthew 7:11 says, "If you, then, though you are evil, know how to give good gifts to your children, how much more will your Father in heaven give good gifts to those who ask him!"

God is the ultimate example for parents. Read the following verses to get a glimpse of His father heart.

Luke 19:41–44

Do you grieve when your children show rebelliousness or a lack of wisdom—even though initially it may look cute or humorous?

Mark 10:17–23 (note v. 21a)

Are you lovingly uncompromising with the truth, even when, at the moment, it is not received?

Hebrews 12:5–11

Do you see God's discipline in your life as positive?

_____

Do you keep the positive end result in the very forefront of your mind when disciplining your children?

_____

Matthew 7:7–11 shows God as a Father who desires to give good gifts to His children. Do you desire to give the good gifts—wisdom, understanding, and maturity—to your children?

_____

Build a Grace-Filled Marriage and Family

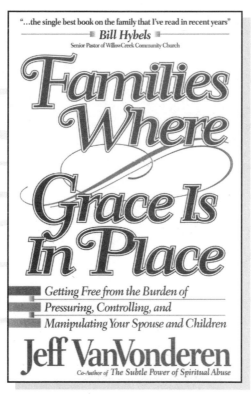

"...the single best book on the family that I've read in recent years"
Bill Hybels
Senior Pastor of WillowCreek Community Church

*C*hristian parents want to do things right. But many end up tired, discouraged and feeling like failures. Healthy relationships are possible only when the filter of God's grace is placed over the processes of marriage and parenting. Jeff VanVonderen gives a message of hope about how God's grace can transform relationships within a marriage and family.

Families Where Grace is in Place by Jeff VanVonderen

BETHANYHOUSE